Secrets of
A Winning Serve
and Return

Secrets of
A Winning Serve and Return

by Peter Talbert
with Lew Fishman

Introduction by Bill Talbert

Photography by
Bruce Curtis

A Stuart L. Daniels Book

PRENTICE-HALL, INC.
Englewood Cliffs, New Jersey

Art Director: Suzanne Esper
Production Consultant: John Storb

SECRETS OF A WINNING SERVE

by Peter Talbert
with Lew Fishman

Copyright © 1977 by
The Stuart L. Daniels Company, Inc.

Published by Prentice-Hall, Inc.
Englewood Cliffs, New Jersey 07632

Printed in United States of America

Prentice-Hall International, Inc., London
Prentice-Hall of Australia, Pty, Ltd., Sydney
Prentice-Hall of Canada, Ltd., Toronto
Prentice-Hall of India Private, Ltd., New Delhi
Prentice-Hall of Japan, Inc., Tokyo

Library of Congress Catalog Card Number: 77-122

ISBN: 0-13-797589-9

For My Mother and Father,
My Brother Pike and Julie,
With All My Love
                    P.T.

Contents

Introduction

John Doeg, the winner at Forest Hills in 1930 and Bob Falkenburg, the Wimbledon champion in 1948, were two players who gained major titles with very little other than a booming serve. This one weapon dominated their games and they used them to full advantage, but their inability to consistently return serves kept them from greatness.

Had they been blessed with what the following stars had, their names would rank higher in tennis history. In 1938, the California redhead Don Budge was the first to win the grand slam of tennis (the championships of Australia, France, England and the United States). He dominated the world tennis scene with his incredible return of serve off both the forehand and backhand. Certainly, his other strokes were there, but this aspect of his game made him invincible.

The same was true about Jack Kramer and Rod Laver at the peak of their greatness. Many young players coming along imitated their fine serves and volleys but failed in the all-important return of serve—that aspect of their games that separated these two giants from the crowd.

Chris Evert and Jimmy Connors, the best of today, win consistently with their returns. Connors, in an interview published in *The New York Times* during the 1977 Aetna Cup matches (U.S. vs. Australia), stated that, given his choice to serve or receive upon winning the toss of the racquet, he preferred to receive. His opponent in the finals, John Alexander, concurred in that this phase of Jimmy's game was the most devastating.

In this new book, *Secrets of A Winning Serve and Return*, Peter Talbert deals with these two all-important tennis strokes in both singles and doubles. He has astutely recognized and written in depth and with clarity about the differences between the two strokes. He has a solid feel for his subject.

Secrets of A Winning Serve and Return is an excellent book, teaching the novice, step by step, how to develop a winning serve. The author then follows with the more difficult task of the return. For the serve, the reader is taught the grip, the stance, feet and weight placement and, finally, execution. I especially enjoyed the well-defined text on the all-important but often neglected toss on the serve.

The book explains in detail the three most used serves in tennis today—flat, spin and American twist. The author employs the clock as his vehicle for understanding this phase of the serve as well as in explaining the return. This kind of graphic description makes for interesting and understandable reading.

I approached the chapter on return of serve with a wary eye. In my opinion this is the most important single shot in tennis. Even if you win all of your services, you must break through your opponent's delivery at least once to win a set. The return of serve is difficult to play consistently and effectively. My wariness disappeared as the subject is handled well. As a matter of fact it helped me win my next Saturday morning doubles match.

The book is not to be read quickly. Digest a small part, try it out on the court and then return to read it again. In this way the detailed sequences of the serve and return can best be absorbed.

Finally, a personal note. I have had many pleasures in my 45 years in tennis but when son Peter asked me to do the introduction for his first book, my pride popped all the strings in my body frame. Thank you, son.

Bill Talbert

Secrets of
A Winning Serve
and Return

1
The Importance of the Serve

The serve is probably the most important single stroke in tennis. I'm sure every tennis player upon taking up the game has heard the adage, "Hold your serve and you'll never lose a match." There are exceptions, of course. Yet 99% of the time the statement does hold water.

The serve *is* the single most devastating stroke in tennis. Used properly and intelligently it can provide the edge that is needed for you to consistently win the majority of your service games. Assuming that you and your opponent are of fairly equal ability the weapon that will give you that important slight advantage is the serve.

By mastering the proper techniques, the serve will start you off on a slightly more offensive note than your opponent. Played properly it can keep you on the offensive throughout all your service games. Never think of it simply as putting the ball in play. Take advantage of your serve. Make it work for you.

Three Basic Serves

There are, as you probably know, three types of basic serves—the flat serve, the American twist and the slice or spin serve. For the player who has left the ranks of beginners I recommend the use of the slice for most serves. It is the most effective and is the serve that will bring you the victories you are looking for. This is not to say that the other serves should not be used at all. As you will see, varying your serve is often good strategy.

All three of the serves will be discussed in detail but I do put emphasis on the slice or spin if you really want to achieve that winning serve.

The principal difference between today's top tennis players and those of the thirties and forties can be stated as a matter of philosophy in the use of the serve. Today, the service is thought of as a bazooka-type weapon. In earlier times the serve was used principally to put the ball into play and the ground strokes were used to win points. Now, one often uses the serve to force a weak return, thereby enabling the server to put his opponent away.

Professionals such as Arthur Ashe and Roscoe Tanner are impressive with their speed and the amount of "kick" they produce, but speed is not necessarily the answer. Such speed does not make their serves more effective than those of other players who achieve their goals with deception and accuracy.

Tennis players who rely on speed entirely find that they have a higher percentage of faults. It is similar to the fastball pitcher who can throw the sphere at greater than one hundred miles an hour, or the home run hitter who can belt the ball out of the park. In each case the player achieves his goal—striking out a batter or hitting a home run—but the pitcher often walks more men than he should, and the hitter strikes out more times than not.

Many average tennis players dream of hitting the ball with the unharnessed power and savagery of the Six Million Dollar Man. This has come about, perhaps, because of the great television coverage major tennis events have received, and the publicity obtained by the pro circuit. Unfortunately those who try to emulate the top players find this ambition detrimental to their game. So just as the fastball pitcher allows too many bases on balls and throws too many wild pitches, the average tennis player with the big serve will double fault far too often for him to be considered a craftsman. He may go home boasting that he aced his opponent three times during the match and while it might make him feel better for the moment, the thought will also penetrate that three aces mean just three points.

As in any sport, consistency pays off. A tennis player must also know himself and his capabilities and be able to play within them. Discipline is important and attention must be paid to the fundamentals.

Build Confidence In Yourself

After you have learned the fundamentals it becomes important to build confidence in your game. This prepares you for the proper mental attitude. In turn, the proper mental attitude will continue to build confidence. The proper mental attitude and the confidence it engenders will bring with it the achievement of control. While this is true in all aspects of the game, nowhere is it more vital than in your serve and return of service.

Never rush your serve. Remember that it is the only tennis stroke in which you control the pace completely. When you're serving you can start whenever you wish, within reason. Take your time.

For example, watch Jimmy Connors play. When he walks back to the baseline he will often bounce the ball six or seven times, very slowly. What he's trying to do is to forget about the previous point. He's establishing a rhythm, relaxing and clearing his mind, getting all set for the next point.

Far too often intermediate level players defeat themselves by dwelling on basic errors. They lose a point and instead of forgetting it, they think about it. They rush back to the baseline, putting unnecessary pressure on themselves, and thus become vulnerable to playing their opponent's game. The rhythm is lost. Try Connors' method to get set for the game ahead. After the match is over, however, analyze your mistakes and think about ways of minimizing them.

Hit Through

A common fault of players who play just a few times a week or less resides in their inability to hit right through the ball on the serve. They stop the racquet after hitting at the ball. Far too much energy is expended in this halting of the downswing. It also negates the arching of the back, the movement of the hips and the upper torso. Such players are hitting the ball exclusively with their arms and are not getting the advantage of the natural, almost automatic drop of the arm and racquet. Consequently, they never develop a comfortable, accurate serve.

Try Jimmy Connors' way of keeping cool by putting the thought of a previous error behind you.

The player with a good service makes it look easy. There is no wasted effort. He is, more than anything else, conscious of the importance of accuracy.

My father (Bill Talbert) is said to have had one of the most effective serves in the game. It was built around pinpoint placement and varying speeds.

In recent years, baseball pitchers have increasingly chosen to pitch without the big, pumping windup. Tennis is similar. The more compact the motion you have with the various parts of your anatomy, the greater your percentage in accomplishing your goal.

For the same reason, it is better to have a relatively slow backswing than a quick, jerky one where you will expend your energies before you even swipe at the ball. This is important if you are to have complete command of your racquet.

Compare this, if you will, to golf. When I took golf lessons my pro told me. "Take your club back very slowly, don't rush it back over your head, take it back slowly and then once you've got it back into the ready position, start to bring it through with some speed." The same applies in tennis.

The intermediate player should spend time thinking about and practicing this kind of control, by which he develops an awareness of every component in the swing.

To prepare himself mentally a player should forget about slamming the ball, or even hitting it. It is far better for him to think about stroking or cradling the ball. One who is able to consider the service this way is at an advantage, since the body will execute movements the mind originates either consciously or unconsciously. The cradling motion is discussed in detail later in this book.

To cure oneself of the "hit" mentality, initially all that is necessary is to begin thinking of an arc, the trajectory one must give to the service. If, upon setting up, the player looks straight at his opponent's service court, he will be looking through the net. If he imagines a straight line drawn from his extended racquet over the net into the service court, he will note a very small area in which to place the ball. He has an equal chance of either going into the net or beyond the service court as he does of putting the ball where it should be. Ostensibly there is only one way a serve can be controlled, allowing for a good margin above the net, some two feet or so, and yet remain within the service box by about three feet. One must envision a downward curve—a sinker ball.

This is not to say one must always have a high looping shot which falls like a dead quail. As you learn to serve correctly, and refinements and adjustments are added to your stroke, you will produce a shot that can clear the net by a safe margin and yet will have pace and forcefulness.

This concept of the arc should dominate one's initial approach to the service. Many good intermediate players ruin their service game by neglecting it. They can hit the ball well, have all the physical movements, but their thinking is misguided. They might go to the line to try to steam a first serve into the box and miss eight out of ten times and have to make it on the second shot. Their problems are strictly mental. They have never thought about the arc concept, and consequently continue to serve as if they were in the beginner category. This, despite the fact that the rest of their game may have progressed significantly over the years.

Possibly it is a matter of ego that drives some tennis players into attempting to clear the net by only a couple of inches each time they are at the baseline. But the only consistency one will be able to derive from this method will be that of disgust and frustration.

Improve Gradually

So, give yourself a break. Don't be so demanding. Improve gradually, with your service being built upon a strong foundation, a solid awareness of the fundamentals.

Allow the ball to clear the net by a good, safe margin. Push the ball out with your racquet as far as your service arm extension will allow, then let the follow-through pull down on the ball. This also puts a lot of the controlling spin on it and you will have started the climb toward a winning serve. The technique of pushing out and the nature of the natural pulling down are discussed later on.

The big, strong fellow will often have a tendency to muscle the ball. It will take far more time for him to realize his machismo is not producing a good service stroke. His swing must be broken down before it can be reconstructed properly.

This is the player who does not feel he can press it out over the net and pull it down into the court. Remember when you are told to pull down into the court you are not consciously trying to pull it down with your arm. Once your racquet has gone out, and followed through the ball as far out as possible, the natural limitations of your arm and the fact that your body is attached to it will naturally start to pull the racquet down. You are not trying to pull it down; the pulling down motion comes automatically. This follow-through action is the most neglected aspect of the service, yet it is one of the most important.

Study Your Opponent

Many players fail to study their foes and remember their tendencies and their vulnerable areas. This should be done because tennis points are won by the ability to force the opposition into errors. The ability to place your adversary on the defensive is a major weapon in your artillery. For example, forcing him into weak, lobbing returns.

If you are playing against a new opponent, try serving the ball directly at him a few times. Observe the direction he moves to make the return . . . which side he favors. Then turn it on . . . to his weaker side.

Another consideration is the physical stature of your foe. Tall players would rather have a bit more room to make the return, gaining leverage from their long arms and sweeping motion. Try to keep the ball right on top of them. Make them feel uncomfortable.

The opposite should be considered for the short player whose arm range is naturally not as long. Try to put the ball as far away from him as you can. Again, there are always exceptions, but these generalities can, for the most part, be accepted.

The only real certainty will be derived after you have served a few balls to the player across the net and have had the opportunity to analyze his reactions.

The Left-Handed Player

Contrary to popular belief, left-handed players are not at a disadvantage in tennis. Particularly in doubles, they may enjoy an advantage. If left-handers realize that right-handers are relatively unaccustomed to playing against left-handed players, while the lefty is constantly doing battle against the righties, he would see the benefits.

A righty playing against a lefty must learn to reverse his entire game and his entire strategy. This requires a great deal of concentration and may result in distracting him from playing his game and cause him to lose control. Against a left-handed player, if you are right-handed, a new dimension

will be added to your game, particularly in doubles where the left-hander will most likely be stationed in the ad court. This is a practice I do not necessarily agree with. You'll be forced to make some changes in your usual techniques.

Put Your Opponent on the Defensive

The key to a winning service is the ability to place your opponent on the defensive. Let him carry the burden. After all, you are the only person on the court who knows where your serve is intended to land.

The ability to deadpan and therefore not telegraph your serve is vital to a good aggressive game. I have heard my father speak of this in great detail. He claims that the lack of that ability is one of the most common faults of the occasional player. I know he worked very hard on this part of his game and perfected it to the point where Australian Davis Cup captain Harry Hopman would have his players constantly watch to see if they could come up with any hint of where he might serve. Actually, dad was forced into this "deception" since he did not have the overwhelming speed of a Pancho Gonzales, a Rod Laver or an Arthur Ashe. He relied a good deal on the elements of surprise and placement.

It is important that a player not develop a definable pattern. For example, a first serve, a slice to the forehand, the second a very soft attempt at the backhand or vice versa. If the man on the other side of the net knows what is coming he no longer is on the defensive. He becomes aggressive and his confidence is buoyed.

Possibly the biggest hurdle you might have to clear at the outset is realizing your limitations, physical as well as mental. There might be some movements your body will just not allow you to perform. It is foolish not to be able to reconcile yourself to these. Each person must learn what is best for him.

Arthur Ashe has just made contact with the ball.
He is snapping his wrist.

Some General Thoughts

I'd like to end this general discussion with these few thoughts.

Tennis should not be considered dissimilar to other everyday movements or activities. Common sense should help you work out many of the components of a tennis swing or tennis strategy. I've mentioned that tennis is similar in some way to playing golf or baseball. There are also other sports with which tennis can be compared. If you have learned the basics of another sport or sports, you'll find some of the principles regarding coordination, timing, practice and other aspects apply to tennis as well.

Tennis is a game of maximization. On serve, with which we are concerned here, trying to maximize height for the angle down in the service court, and a maximization of spin for the clearance of the net and control.

Try also to find that middle ground between power, the speed with which one hits the ball, and control, which is in the spin. Continually try to maximize your percentages which means the number of times you clear the net and place the ball in the court to which you are directing it.

A ball hit with power alone may occasionally ace your opponent. But every miss that means the use of a second serve is harmful. To serve one ace and four second serves out of five points is bad tennis and leads to a losing match. Faced constantly with second serves your opponent will relax and gain confidence. But he'll be pressing if the first serve always goes in. Like a pitcher who is always ahead of the count, it gives him leeway, and cuts down the batter's options. Going for an ace occasionally is okay but make sure it fits into your plan for the match. If you do go for an ace, ask yourself if it sets up future possibilities.

Remember to vary your speed, your spin, and your placement. Always, always, a maximization of your abilities.

========

As you will notice, from time to time I refer to the spin serve as the slice serve because I feel the two terms are interchangeable, so please don't be confused about this terminology.

Also to be considered is the fact that just as 90% of the population is right handed, 90% of tennis players are too. Therefore, most of my references are to the right hander. Those who are lefties will have to reverse the instructions dealing with the use of the right or left hand which I'm sure they have already become used to doing.

Everything I have written here applies to women players as well as men but more often than not I have used the masculine pronoun as it is quite awkward to be continually referring to "he or she."

2
Equipment

There are times when I think people pay more attention to owning prestige equipment items than they do to their game. However, properly fitted equipment does make a difference.

How often have you gone into a sporting goods store to buy a can of balls and watched players swishing a racquet through the air, putting it back on the rack, trying another, returning to the first, etc. To the uninitiated it might appear that they are a bit mentally deranged, but they are looking for something that will "work" for them. One of the major requisites in selecting one piece of equipment over another is that you believe in the one you choose and feel comfortable with it.

If you have confidence in your equipment you are a step closer to gaining an edge over the fellow who just picks up any old war club with which to do battle.

Choosing a Racquet

It is impossible to generalize to help you in the selection of a racquet since the most important requisite is comfort. What feels good to one person might not be right for another. That is why it is important to try out a number of racquets.

Aside from personal preference there are three basic factors to consider in the choice of a racquet which is the single most important piece of equipment you will buy.

The weight of the available racquets varies from 12 to 15 ounces. Two interesting exceptions were the racquets used by Dick Savitt and Don Budge, both of whom used racquets weighing more than 16 ounces (Savitt's with a grip size of 5⅛ inches). Naturally, the heavier the implement the more force you will be able to impart to the ball. This does not mean that everyone attempting to upgrade his equipment should be searching for a bludgeon.

The range of three ounces sounds almost insignificant, but when a person has a grooved stroke, moving up or down the scale just one ounce may play havoc with the rhythm and timing. The results obtained from a difference in weight are so noticeable that some players will switch to a lighter racquet when they feel fatigued.

I personally do not recommend this. I believe that you should use one racquet, become accustomed to it and to what you can expect to do with it. Since you should think of the racquet as an extension of your arm, it should always feel comfortable.

Weight of the Racquet

Choose a racquet with enough weight for you, but one you will always be able to control, one which will not drain your energy halfway through a grueling match.

The most common mistake made in buying a racquet is getting one that is too heavy. Usually when you walk into a pro shop, you are fresh and have greater strength than you would after an hour or so of exertion. The racquet "feels" good and strong. You buy it. Then, after playing with it for an hour or more, you begin to think there is a lead weight inserted at the throat.

Possibly one of the best ways to purchase a racquet is to turn to your professional for guidance, or enter his shop after your match is completed. See what feels good then.

Without attempting to pigeonhole you, let me say that most youths use the 12 ounce variety, while women tend to favor a racquet approximately an ounce heavier. A man usually uses a weaopn in the 13½ to 14 ounce range, or more, depending on his physical attributes. The great Aussie Rod Laver used a 13 ounce evenly balanced racquet.

There are several other matters to consider in selecting your racquet. For example, what type of surface are you going to be playing on? If you usually play on a clay court you can use any kind of racquet, light to heavy, because you will have a fair amount of time to react on most of your shots. If you play mostly on fast surfaces such as a hard court or a grass court you should be thinking about getting a lighter racquet, one which you can quickly move around. If you use a heavy racquet on these surfaces the chances are you'll end up hitting the ball late in a lot of instances. In the same vein when you play on fast surfaces you might think about using a metal racquet which has less wind resistance and which you can swing around a lot faster than a wooden racquet.

The Right Grip Size

Equally as important as weight is the grip size, or the circumference. Handles are made in various shapes and your selection is once again a personal matter. Since you'll have to control the racquet, you must be able to get your hand around the handle.

The best way to choose the grip size which is right for you is to grasp the handle in your hand and then have your thumb overlap the nail of your middle finger. If your nail is covered by your thumb the grip is probably the proper size. But again, most of all, it must feel comfortable. You have to live with it.

There are various pitfalls. If the handle is too thick, you will not be able to get a firm grip on it. You also will have difficulty in constantly adjusting your grip after each shot during the course of a match. If the grip is not big enough, there is a tendency to hold the racquet rather loosely and the result is a complete loss of control. The racquet will always be turning in your hand.

Another variable which should be taken into consideration is balance. That is, between the weight of the head and that of the handle. It is what golf professionals pride themselves on . . . swingweight, as opposed to deadweight or overall weight.

Only the more advanced players and professionals are able to calibrate this type of measurement themselves. Most players will need help in finding the properly balanced racquet, one that is neither too heavy in the head nor in the handle.

If you attempt to calculate this yourself, take into consideration the length of the racquet, which is approximately 27 inches. Place your index finger under the racquet, at the center. Most racquets have a variable of approximately one-half inch either way.

Stringing

The third factor in the choice of racquets is the material with which it is strung. Nylon and animal gut are the most common types. Nylon is used in most ready-strung racquets. It stands up much longer than gut because it does not absorb moisture as readily.

I recommend using nylon if you are a beginner or if you play in an area that has a lot of moisture in the air, say near the sea. A number of players have one racquet strung with nylon for use on a wet court after a rain.

If you play a great deal of tennis, gut stringing can give you a little added response because it has a flexibility which nylon does not have. There is a bit more give in this type of stringing. The ball will feel better. I also recommend gut if you have arm problems. Being a more rigid material, nylon will put an added strain on your elbows.

The pros and world class players seek lamb's gut for their stringing material. They feel it offers them a bit more "bite" on their shots. But gut is not as durable as nylon, not to mention more expensive.

However, if tennis has become a way of life for you, that is, if you play three or more times a week and want the best possible equipment, opt for gut.

If you are not buying your racquet "off the rack" and are having one strung, you should make certain that the material is pulled tight enough, that it will no longer stretch. The pressure chosen by most players is from approximately 58 to 63 pounds.

I personally prefer a racquet strung fairly loosely, and I usually have my racquets strung at around 53 pounds. I find that this lets the ball stay on my racquet a little longer. With the added contact time I have better control of the ball.

Again, with relation to playing surfaces, if you are playing on faster surfaces you might want to have your racquet strung a little bit looser than you would when playing on the slower surfaces. When that ball comes at you rapidly and you therefore have less control of it, if you can keep it on your strings a bit longer, it will take something off the speed and you'll gain greater control.

You will probably also take into consideration the symmetry of the racquet, the cosmetic look.

Metal or Wood

There then remains the matter of whether you should choose a metal racquet (aluminum or an alloy) or one made of wood. The intermediate player will probably play just as well or just as poorly with either. This is not to say there are no differences. There most definitely are, but most fall within the confines of practicality. For example, a metal racquet will probably last longer and need less maintenance than a wooden racquet which has a tendency to warp or splinter. The metal racquet does not need a press and will store better. The fact that it is easier to swing may be a boon to some players.

Pros endorse both the wooden and the metal racquets, and you see an increasing number changing to the metal variety, but many believe metal has too much of a slingshot or trampoline effect.

It's not possible to have as much control with metal as with wood, because the racquet moves too fast through the hitting area and overpowers the ball, taking away from accuracy.

The pros also believe the wooden racquets have more *feel* at impact, that they can move the ball better. However, I believe that the player just getting involved should give the metal a try . . . even the graphite racquet or the new oversized racquet.

I believe that the oversize racquet could be one of the important innovations in tennis. The larger size of the face of the racquet and the increased area of the sweet spot makes it an excellent racquet for those just starting to play or for those in the upper age brackets whose eyes are not as sharp and movements not as rapid as they once were. Both categories of players will be taking more shots off center so that the added sweet spot area will make the play a lot easier and more gratifying.

Selecting the Ball

Not as important as your selection of a racquet but worthy of consideration is the choice of the tennis balls you are going to use. There are many popular brands on the market. Most of them come in sealed pressurized tins. The United States Tennis Association has approved about a dozen different labels.

Different balls are manufactured for the various playing surfaces as well as for night competition and present a broad spectrum of color which makes it easier to follow the flight.

Too many players keep their balls in play long after they are worn out. Naturally, I don't expect you to use a different trio after every match as those on the top professional tours do. But it is important that you do not continue to play with a ball after the surface material has worn off in one spot or another. Watch out for the kind of light ball used sometimes by beginners. It could hurt your stroking pattern because it will bounce too high, or travel too far. Stay with good balls and by that I mean those which when dropped from a height that is level with your jaw will bounce no higher than your waistline.

The exception to this rule is if you are a beginner and have not played very much. As a beginner it might be a good idea to use a ball which is slightly dead, which has lost some of its pressure. This will make the ball a lot slower. It will also mean

that the ball will stay in play longer since a livelier ball has a tendency to fly all over. So, if you are a beginner, try playing with slightly dead balls to help you prolong your rallys and add to your confidence in controlling the ball. Also, you can slow down older balls by sandpapering them to increase the fuzziness of the surface.

For the player who has left the beginner classification, I suggest using only good balls, even in practice. Practice, after all, is simulation of a real game and your conditions should be similar.

Tennis Dress

I am not going to pursue the matter of tennis dress in too great detail except to say that it is highly important that your clothing and shoes feel comfortable.

Perhaps something that happened to one of the members of the World Team Tennis Boston Lobsters will illustrate what I mean. The clothing the Lobsters wear on the court is provided by a certain manufacturer. The manufacturer decided that the usual cut of the traditional tennis shorts looked too baggy and were not too attractive. He decided to cut them very slim to fit snugly. As one of the male members of the team was stretching for a point during a match his pants split wide open causing him, shall we say, a bit of embarrassment. So keep your clothing loose and comfortable and not necessarily snug.

White is still the accepted traditional color for shorts, tops, socks, and sneakers. But, as you know, tennis clothing in colors and designer styles has arrived on the scene with a much wider range of all types of outfits for the fashion-conscious man or woman. Use your judgment but remember to follow the rules of the courts on which you are playing.

Virginia Wade playing in one of the newer tennis outfits.

As far as shoes are concerned, I believe one gets greater comfort from those with leather uppers rather than the standard canvas variety. The leather breathes and thus helps ease burning feet. Cushion soles also help absorb some of the pounding on modern surfaces. The other aspect to consider is that leather shoes are much more durable than canvas, although they also are far more expensive.

When you purchase a pair of tennis shoes, do exactly that. Don't settle for sneakers used in basketball or any other sport. Make sure the shoes you buy are light, comfortable and have treads on the sole. The latter will give you far better traction on the court. Also be certain when you try on the shoes that you first don a pair of wool tennis socks, or two, if that is what you wear when playing. In doing this, you avoid the problem of blisters.

At any rate, do feel comfortable in what, and with what you are playing.

Stan Smith has made contact with the ball. His feet are in the air and he is leaning forward, getting ready to come towards the net.

3
The Grip

The grip, like a handshake, can mirror one's style. Often, when you shake hands with a person you try to learn something about him. A quick, hearty handshake seems to denote confidence and strength. A limp hand with a weak grip seems to reflect a lack of stamina or aggressiveness. Shaking hands is one way of summing up another person's character. This also carries over onto the tennis court.

Your opponent will be studying your grip, trying to figure out your approach and strategy. At the same time you should be analyzing his. Racquet control begins with the grip. It dictates the way you manipulate your weapon. Since the racquet is an extension of your arm, the type of grip used can signal one's strengths and weaknesses. In part it's the grip that can determine whether your serves will be flat sweeping drives or curling lashes into the box.

Once one progresses beyond the elementary stages of being able to consistently clear the net and serve into the box, all else becomes a matter of control and discipline. This means learning the relationship between various grips and the spins placed on the ball. The more you are able to direct the spin, the more effective your service, because a ball hit with spin is not as easily read as a ball hit flat.

Essentially, your grip will evolve along the lines of what feels comfortable to you and the kind of serve you are trying to hit. When I refer to comfort, I mean that grip which enables you to hit the ball with uniformity and rhythm—the grip that works for you.

The Three Basic Grips

The three basic grips—Eastern, Western and Continental —differ mainly in the position of the V, the outline made by the thumb and forefinger on the handle of a racquet held straight in front of you with the face vertical. While the difference in position may be slight, the resulting alterations can substantially affect the spin placed on the ball and, thus, the direction and speed of your serve.

Only two of the grips, the Eastern and Continental, are considered service grips while the Western, which has been used for forehand strokes, is largely out of style now. The Eastern and Continental, and variations of both, are used for the forehand, backhand and overhead strokes as well. A fourth grip is the backhand grip, not suitable for the serve. While we are here concentrating on the service grips, it seems desirable to look at all four in the light of an overall view of control.

Getting Started

Let us first discuss certain points that are the same for all three grips.

A good practice routine when you're learning to serve is to choke up on the racquet so that your hand is almost on the throat of the racquet, perhaps just three or four inches below the face. Once you have studied the mechanics of the swing and know how to get your toss up and what the swing of the racquet should be like, start out your practice sessions by using the abbreviated grip. Toss the ball up quite low and get the feeling of swinging through. The reason for doing this is that most beginners have trouble orienting themselves to hitting a ball with a racquet that is two feet long. Hand to eye coordination is difficult anyway. But placing a racquet in your hand that is approximately 27 inches in length and then tossing the ball up and trying to hit it with that extension is difficult at first. So at the start make it easy on yourself and choke up. Gradually work your way down the handle until your hand is on the grip.

The reason for doing this is that you'll find your power increase with the length of your reach. If this seems uncomfortable initially, start at a point on the racquet handle which does seem natural and then work on lowering your hand to the racquet butt as you develop control and strength.

A Two-Handed Proposition

Another point to remember is that the grip, regardless of the style, is a two-handed proposition. The right hand may actually hold the racquet and carve out the strokes, but it's the left hand that cradles the racquet throat and shifts the racquet

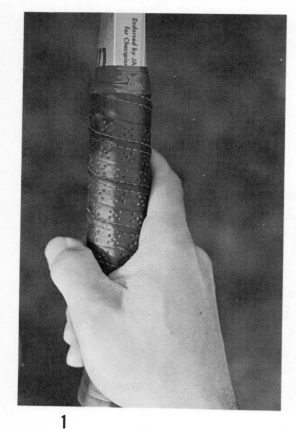

1

 2

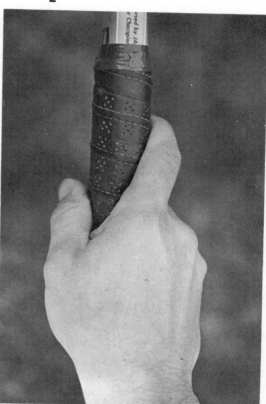

3

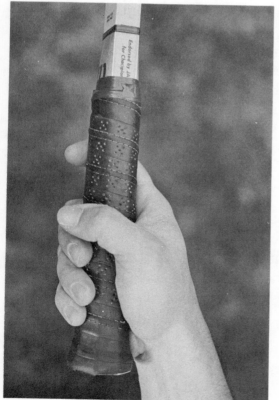

The three basic grips. (1) The Eastern Grip. The V formed by the thumb and forefinger is centered on top of the handle or a slight bit to the left. Grasp the racquet as if you were shaking hands. Notice that the left bevel extends right into the V formed by thumb and forefinger. (2) The Continental Grip. Here the V formed by the hand is to the left of the left bevel. (3) The Western Grip. The V of the hand is to the right, on the right bevel. For accuracy start at the top of the photos where the bevels are clearly seen and trace a line to the hand.

in your hand. You should not move your hand in changing grips; move only the racquet.

How the grip feels becomes a matter of personal style. Obviously, your fingers must hold the racquet firmly, but this pressure should be evenly divided among your fingers and they all should remain loose enough to "feel" the racquet. Finally, your grip should be considered a lock, the means of making your racquet an extension of your arm and wrist.

The Eastern and Western grips are purely American in origin and the Continental, as the name implies, came into being in England and Europe in the early years of tennis. The American grips seem to have evolved to compensate for the hardness of the balls. The relatively high compression of balls manufactured in the United States required a grip that would keep the wrist behind the racquet and help hold the balls down.

The Western Grip

This was particularly true with the Western grip, in which the racquet is closed, with the top the leading edge. This was needed to compensate for the concrete surfaces and high bounces that characterized tennis in the western part of the United States.

The Western, used the least of all the grips, represents one extreme—the V is on the right bevel of the racquet handle pointing toward the right shoulder. The wrist is solidly behind the handle.

The Western forehand produces a ripping topspin, a strenuous style whose most visible exponents today are Bjorn Borg and Harold Solomon. In the forehand, this topspin—which has the ball spinning forward in the same direction as it is travelling—is useful in handling high balls but it is very limiting in returning balls hit low unless one can slice underneath them. In short, it's fairly awkward, tiring to use, and limited in function. It is rarely used to execute backhands or serves.

The Eastern Grip

The Eastern lies midway between the Western and the Continental. It, too, evolved with a purpose. The Eastern was born on the clay courts of the east coast of the United States where one did not want the severely closed racquet face of the Western nor the open face of the Continental. As one can surmise, in the standard Eastern, the racquet face is vertical. The V formed by the thumb and forefinger is centered on top of the handle's surface or a little to the left of it.

For beginners, the Eastern grip is considered the most comfortable and easiest to control. It is the most natural way to hold the racquet and is referred to as the "shake hands" grip.

The advantage of the Eastern grip is that it allows you to hit a fairly flat, straight serve with a minimum of spin. This gives beginners the best immediate results, enabling them to then concentrate on developing the other mechanics of the game. The Eastern serve is relatively simple to master.

To form the standard Eastern grip, hold the throat of the racquet in your left hand and rest the butt of the racquet on the heel of your right hand. Now firmly grasp the racquet as if you were "shaking hands." Your fingers should be slightly curved and your index finger should extend a bit toward the throat. Along with the thumb, your forefinger should curl diagonally across the grip. Your palm is on the same line as the flat of the handle, and your forearm, wrist and racquet form a straight line.

Make sure that the shaft of the racquet does not form an angle with your wrist and your forearm. If this happens chances are that your fingers will start to pull together and you will be gripping the racquet more like a club and therefore have less area under your control. The more you can spread your fingers out over the racquet the better control you will have over it—the more it will feel as though it is entirely a part of your hand.

Your wrist should be locked during the swing and your grip is firm when the strings hit the ball.

Another way to envision the Eastern is to start with the Western grip and then, with the left hand holding the throat, move the handle a quarter turn to the right.

The Eastern grip, with the racquet face vertical and the V along the topside of the racquet, results in a flat service which is sometimes used for the first serve. (As you will note later, I am not in favor of using the flat serve very often.) The reason for using a flat serve only on a first serve is that the hard flat serve is the most difficult to control. It is simply too risky to try it on the second serve when accuracy is a must.

The Continental Grip

Once you have mastered the Eastern and are sure of a swift, straight shot into the service box, it's time to put an arc into the sphere's trajectory. It's time to add spin, the essential ingredient for a well-controlled serve designed to deceive your opponent. This means it's time to move to the Continental, the grip primarily used by the pros in serving, and the grip every advanced amateur should ultimately strive to master.

The reason most tournament players favor the Continental is understandable. It's the only service grip that is flexible enough to use on any serve—flat, slice or twist—and it also has the potential for maximum power through a whip-like motion of the wrist and the transference of body weight for maximum control. But first one must master control for, without it, power is useless.

The Continental grip evolved in England where grass courts tended to result in low bounces. Consequently, the Continental's open face with the bottom of the racquet being the leading edge, was required to lift the ball up and over the net. The grip is also good for the backhand and is sometimes referred to as the Eastern backhand. For the forehand, though, it leaves something to be desired. The Continental gives good position for hitting low, bouncing balls, but is awkward for hitting high ones, where it decreases strength and control. But for the service, it is the grip to which one should aspire.

In the Continental, the V made by the thumb and forefinger is just to the left of the left bevel. The heel of the thumb of your right hand rests on top of the handle and the thumb stretches around to the left. Your forefinger still wraps diagonally upwards around the handle, with the knuckle resting on the right bevel.

The Continental service grip is approximately halfway between the Eastern forehand and backhand grips. The wrist rests somewhat below the racquet head and instead of the straight line formed by the wrist, arm and racquet, there is now a very slight break or angle formed at the wrist.

Each increased turn toward the Continental grip increases the slice on the serve, and thus, the arc put on the ball. However, it is wise to change from the Eastern to the Continental very slowly—really just a fraction at a time—because a minor change in the angle of the grip can bring a dramatic change to the spin on the ball. Take your time.

Observe how an adjustment of the racquet alters the ball's arc. Basically, a serve hit with spin will allow you to aim higher over the net, as the slicing motion pulls down the ball once it has cleared.

This is the most important reason for using the Continental grip. Once again let me emphasize that in the game of tennis you should be thinking about maximizing your percentages. If the Continental is the grip that allows you to put more spin on the ball and that, in turn, allows you to clear the net more often, thereby increasing your chances of getting the serve in, that is the grip you should be using. Maximize.

Since the slice serve is the easiest to learn to control, it tends to be relied on for the service. The slicing motion or curve makes it difficult for your opponent to judge the path and speed of the ball. In general, the greater the slice, the harder it is to "measure" the serve.

The Backhand Grip

The backhand grip, rarely used on the serve, is primarily utilized for hitting backhand ground strokes and for a backhand return of serve. Very few top tournament players even use it as it imparts extreme spin, almost more than is needed. It is at the other end of the spectrum from the Western grip.

To produce the backhand grip, hold the racquet straight out in front of you. With your right hand find the second bevel to the left and place this into the "V" of your hand. This means that your thumb will be almost completely in back of the racquet. It will be running along the flat edge that is on the left side of the racquet. You can feel the power that this would give you for a backhand stroke. However, you will feel how awkward it would be in using it to hit a forehand. It would also be awkward on the serve.

Hold the racquet over your head as though you were about to hit a ball on the service motion. Notice the direction in which the hitting face of the racquet is aiming—it is almost back towards you. This means that you must turn your wrist in an extreme fashion to get the face open enough to make contact with the ball. This is tough to do for many players. For this reason I do not recommend it for the service motion. Stay with something less extreme which, in my opinion, is the Continental grip.

The Grip on Forehand and Backhand

Obviously, forehand and backhand strokes are played with opposite sides of the racquet. If backhand strokes are made with a forehand grip, they tend to push the ball, shortchanging you on power. To demonstrate this to yourself, look at how much of your hand is behind the racquet when you're hitting a forehand.

Now, take the racquet to your backhand side and see how much is in back of it. Instead of having the back of your hand behind, you now only have the tips of four fingers. There's very little grip behind the racquet to enable you to hit the ball with any power. Again to prove the point move the racquet to your forehand side and push against something solid. You should be able to push quite hard with the racquet. Reverse it, take it to the backhand side and again push against something solid. The racquet will almost feel as if it is pushing back in your hand. The same thing will happen when a ball comes to your racquet. When it makes contact instead of you controlling it, pushing the racquet through, the ball will more likely move the racquet in your hand and you will have lost control.

Let me emphasize that changing the way a racquet rests in your hand even the slightest degree means you are altering the course of the ball. Start with a flat Eastern grip and move the racquet a fraction to the right toward the Continental or a hair to the left toward the Western and you're adding either slice or topspin, respectively. The effect of this on shot placement is discussed in the chapter on the swing.

Regardless of the names given the various positions, the important thing is how the grip feels and how well you are able to control the racquet. As you progress, you probably will wind up favoring a grip that falls somewhere between the standard Eastern and Continental grips.

Of course, ideally, you should have a complete repertoire of service grips in your arsenal—all degrees of Eastern and Continental to vary the extent of the "kick" placed on the ball. And ideally, you should be able to mix them up in such a way as to best psyche out your opponent.

Remember, while you're trying to confound him, he's going to be keeping his eye on you. And he may be checking your grip to see whether he can expect the hard flat serve of an Eastern or the downward curling motion of the Continental's slice. Certainly, he's going to try to anticipate. And so should you.

4
Stance and Footwork

Footwork. It's the key to success in so many sports. In baseball, it's the power behind the batted ball and the timing and agility needed to catch it. It's critical in basketball. Just think of the nature of the timing and balance behind the ability to fake, pivot, and jump. In boxing, the preoccupation with dancing in the ring is certainly justified as the opponent is set up.

Tennis is no exception. Your stance and footwork will be a major factor in the balance, timing and power in your serve as well as your effectiveness in the return.

No matter how clever you are or how devastating your stroke, it won't mean much unless you can get to the ball on time. And getting there is not enough, either. Proper footwork is a means of making every shot as easy to play as possible.

When you watch an Arthur Ashe or a Chris Evert you get the impression that they neither rush their footwork nor their stroke. They simply appear to be in the right place at the right time. This seeming ease and fluidity is the result of endless practice and is the mark of a top player.

The breathlessness of the beginner is due in large measure to his inability to direct his feet to the proper point on the court at the proper time. Bad timing is in good part brought about by poor footwork.

One might think that footwork and balance would be fairly easy to master. After all, walking, running, skipping, dancing—we have been doing these our entire lives. And these movements are what you are basically doing on the court. They should be natural. And in a sense they are. But unless one has been active in other sports, the basics of footwork must be studied. You can't leave it to instinct.

Some Basics

There are two basic rules, and although they are among the first a beginner learns, it's important to reiterate them. Unless you are in tune with the basics it's impossible to progress. The first rule is to wait for a stroke facing the net, with your body parallel to it. The second is, as much as possible, to hit every ball with your hips and shoulders sideways or at right angles to the net. This is the case for every shot: service, return, ground stroke, lob, volley, overhead.

There also are some fundamentals that apply specifically to stances and footwork. For instance, your knees should always be slightly bent, giving you a springy flexible feeling rather than one that is straight and rigid. Also, you should keep most of your weight on the balls of your feet. Quick reflexes or a fast

Chris Evert has the ability to be in the right place at the right time.

John Newcombe's racquet has reached the prime position. Notice that he is on the toe of his left foot, his body is extremely extended, preparatory to going up and out towards the ball.

start hinge on being ready to go, with the best balance achieved by coming off the ball of the foot.

Skipping and Shuffling

Another fundamental move is skipping, and I don't particularly mean the grammar school variety either. This is a simple but important motion that will give you lateral movement. It is a quick movement to reach the ball when it is only one or two steps away.

When you must move to your right, move your right foot to the right lightly dragging your left foot with it. Keep going in this fashion. If you are moving to your left, move your left foot and pull your right foot with it, the reverse of the move to the right.

If, for instance, you were to turn and run to the right rather than moving in this fashion you would be then out of position to move swiftly to your left if the next ball should be returned on that side. A low crab-like skip or shuffle can often move you very fast, as can be seen in the movements of top fencers.

The Service Stance

Now that we have cleared the decks of some of the basics, let us consider the service stance.

First, take the time to set up properly. Don't rush yourself or your opponent. If you hurry most likely you will throw your timing off. If you try to pull a fast one on your opponent with a quick serve, it will not only be bad sportsmanship but it can result in a call on you for a "let ball". The point would then be replayed.

So pause. When you are serving is the one chance you have to set the pace of the game and you stand to gain the most from it. Think of what you want to do then get ready to do it. Keep calm. I know that's difficult, especially when your thoughts run to unleashing an ultimate display of power and accuracy. It's similar to a golfer staying cool and moving with care as he prepares to tee off on the first hole. Unfortunately, most of us usually don't settle down until the first few pace-setting moments are behind us.

The positioning of your feet is crucial to the serve since this is the source from which you draw balance and power. To prove this try serving with both your feet close together. Hit the ball; you'll find that the only power you get will be from your arms. You must spread your feet apart in order to get the power to be derived from your legs, hips, and shoulders.

In serving to your opponent's forehand court, stand approximately one foot to the right of the center mark on the baseline and several inches behind it.

Those few inches will avoid foot faulting should you creep forward during the service motion. Both feet must remain behind the baseline. You cannot cross the line into your court until after you hit the ball. If you do, you commit a foot fault.

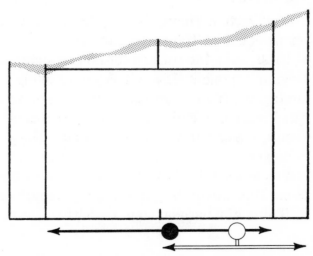

Where to stand to serve for singles and doubles. Black circle for singles. Open circle for doubles. Note in each case the server has divided the court he must cover approximately in half.

Place your left foot in front of your right foot. Your left foot should be angled about 45 degrees toward the baseline, pointing toward the right net post. Your right foot should be placed approximately some 14 inches behind your left, parallel to the baseline. Your right foot also should be slightly further to the right than your left so that if you drew a line from toe to toe, it would point in the direction of the service court at which you are aiming. For a left-handed player this foot placement obviously is reversed.

Keep your knees flexed slightly. Bounce a bit on your toes. Is your position comfortable? If you feel that moving your right foot back another inch or so will give you better balance, by all means, do so. There are no unalterable rules. Your stance should feel natural to you.

Where to Stand

While thoughts differ on how close one should stand to the baseline when serving, it makes sense to stand as close as you can without foot faulting. The better players are right close up there. Since the service is the big gun in today's game, if called for you should be prepared to follow each serve up to the net and volley the return.

Remember also that with every inch or two you move further away from the baseline you decrease the angle of the trajectory of the ball over the net. This then reduces the chances of hitting the ball into the service box. Stay as close to the line as you can without foot faulting and you maximize your chances of getting your serve in.

Since you don't know yet the place where your opponent will be returning your serve, it is also logical to stand as close to the center mark as you can. In that way you're prepared to go either right or left.

An Exception to Make

There is a time when you might want to take a position a foot or two away from the center mark and that is when you are trying to angle your serve wide to the corner of either the forehand or the backhand service box. Positioning yourself nearer the sideline even slightly will increase the angle of your trajectory to these two areas. Otherwise, stay close to the center.

In doubles play an adjustment is made by moving even further towards the sideline. When you have a partner you should stand halfway between the center baseline mark and the doubles sideline of your court. This puts you in the best spot to cover your half of the court.

Returning the Serve

When you are in the receiving position and preparing to return a serve it is important that you take a "ready stance". After you have played tennis for a while, falling into the ready position is almost instinctive.

Here are some guidelines. Stand behind the baseline facing the net with your legs spread apart and your feet more or less lined up with the position of your shoulders. What you are trying to achieve is good balance. Your knees should be slightly bent and your weight evenly distributed on the balls of your feet. Don't stand flat-footed.

Your racquet should be pointed towards the net with your right hand gripping the handle easily while your left hand lightly cradles the throat. The head of the racquet should be just slightly higher than your wrist.

To return the serve properly you must be aware of the basics involved in proper footwork in order to be able to transfer your weight and thus put power into your stroke. The key to this is a forward motion into and through the ball. This is the only way you can get your weight into the shot. Advance your left foot for a forehand shot and your right foot for the backhand. (It should be noted that this "stepping in" motion is only possible against a serve where you have a reasonable amount of time, when you are not rushed. Otherwise you should use the open stance, for which see below.)

Correct forehand footwork entails having your left foot pointed forward at an angle of about 45 degrees, somewhat as in the service stance. Your knee is flexed. Your right foot is braced and prepared to shove your weight through the swing and onto your left foot. Sometimes a player will look as if he has the right position but.he has moved into it by putting his right foot back rather than moving his left ahead. This is self-defeating because the leverage achieved by stepping into a stroke is then lost. The perfectly timed shot is one that is hit at the very moment that the weight shifts.

Even if you are forced to run backwards to reach a ball, shift your weight forward or at least brace yourself as you actually make the shot.

The Open and Closed Stance

There is a difference of opinion on the merits of the closed stance as contrasted with the open stance. In the closed stance one foot is in front of another in a manner similar to the service stance. In the open stance you're facing the net as you make your shot moving your right foot sideways for a forehand shot and your left for a backhand shot. Both stances have their assets and liabilities. The open stance will give you a faster recovery after the shot while the closed position provides you with a bit more power.

With an open stance the leverage needed to put power into your shot is provided by turning your shoulders and torso. Your feet really have nothing to do with this but your shoulders must turn. It provides you with the leverage so necessary to make sure that you play the ball and that the ball does not play you. Top professional players use both stances depending upon the circumstances. It is important to remember to be flexible in the many aspects of tennis and not to fall into an unyielding pattern. Very often the way to go is with what feels right and works for you.

In a later chapter dealing specifically with the return of serve, I will be discussing in detail the open stance return because I believe this to be the more useful.

In returning a wide, low ball, hit to your forehand, take your last step with your right foot, moving into an open position which tends to lift the ball. This is a very important rule. Always try to use your right foot in taking that last step for a very wide forehand. It will help you to start moving back to the center of the court at almost the same moment you're swinging at the ball. It's vital to make a rapid recovery.

Some Other Points

There are some other footwork skills that are important to bear in mind. For one, do not, if you can possibly avoid it, cross your legs. If you want to see how difficult this makes your play, try to step into a shot with one leg over the other while remaining parallel to the net. You just can't.

Instead of doing this, skip short distances so that you will be able to advance the proper foot when moving into the ball. A number of quick steps, skips and short hops are preferable to long strides. This way you will always have your weight on the balls of your feet, poised and ready to go. Long strides can throw you off balance.

I have always admired Leslie Turner Bowrie, a woman player from "down under" who is able to do this better than anyone I have ever seen. Her steps were always very short and choppy and she moved so well.

Another point to remember is that in running for a ball only the legs move in this sport. In basketball a player will pump his arms as he runs. The arms of a tennis player, however, must be used to hold the racquet and be kept in the ready position.

Proper footwork also requires that you bend low to hit a low shot. Not doing this is the reason even good players sometimes have trouble handling low shots. In such a shot your knee will almost be touching the court.

You may not think that it will make a difference in your game but being able to bend low can be very effective. Try to have your center of gravity on the same level as that of the ball. Don't stand above the ball. Get down with it. You'll see it better. When you shift your weight in to hit the ball you'll be shifting it at the same level. This is comparable to the difference between aiming a gun through the gunsight and shooting it from your hip. You obviously have greater control when you are sighting it and the same will be true in tennis.

5

The Toss

A consistent, accurate toss is vital to produce a good service. The purpose of the toss is to place the ball in the line of flight of the racquet face.

You should not attempt to maneuver your service motion swing to where you've tossed the ball, if the ball isn't in its precise position. There is only one natural and effective service motion, and from which you'll be getting the most out of every part of your body. What you must do on the toss is to put the ball in the place where the face of the racquet will be naturally swinging through. There is little to be realized from a bad toss. It will only cut down on your effectiveness and reduce your percentage of accurate serves.

I sometimes think that the toss is the most difficult part of the game to master and yet most players tend to give it the least attention.

If there is one independent thought that puts a player off, it is forgetting that a toss is not a throw. It is more like a push. It is this feeling of pushing or raising the ball up that one must bear in mind.

There is no reason to hurry your toss. Take your time. To loosen up, you might want to try a few practice tosses. That;s fine.

If you are a right-handed player the ball should be held lightly between the thumb and first two fingers of your left hand and about waist high. Don't grasp the ball in the palm of your hand or it will be difficult to release. The left-hander, of course, holds the ball in his right hand.

Unless you are engaged in a tournament and have ball boys to throw you a second ball, you should serve with two balls in your hand. The second ball is held between your last two fingers and the palm of your hand. If you find doing this unwieldy or disconcerting to your game, try a tennis outfit with pockets big enough to hold a ball.

The Technique of the Toss

On the toss, your left elbow should be reasonably close to your waist. Your forearm should be parallel to the ground and pointed in the same direction as your left foot.

Drop your forearm slightly so that it is pointing towards the ground. Then move your arms up as you coordinate with the swing which is discussed in the next chapter.

As you go through this motion, think about easing the ball up, pushing it, hanging it up there. These motions should become second nature. Include it consciously among your checkpoints. If not, natural inclinations will take over and you will tend to throw the ball up. A proper toss is not a natural motion and must be thought about until mastered.

Release the ball only when your hand is over your head. Visualize pushing the ball up a very narrow elevator shaft. This should help avoid looping arcs from right to left, or front to back which would only have an adverse effect on your serve.

For the slice serve, the proper height of the toss is to the center or slightly higher than the center of the racquet when it is held in a fully extended right arm. This is approximately three feet over your head and a foot and one-half in front of you.

The ball goes up and reaches its apex. The racquet has been cocked back and is ready. If the strings of the racquet hit the ball as it is momentarily stopped in mid-air, at its highest point, then you will savor the joy of perfect timing.

It is easier to hit a target that is still than one that is moving. But to get that ball to "hang" takes practice.

Practicing the Toss

Here is how you go about practicing the toss for the slice serve. To work towards perfecting your toss so that it "hangs" at the right point, stand facing a wall or backboard approximately one yard from it. Extend your racquet to its full height and note where the tip is in relation to the wall. Mark that place on the wall with some masking tape. Now practice with the hand you'll use for the toss (left for right-handers, right for lefties).

Toss the ball up. Does it hit the wall? Or is it over your head or farther away from it than you are? If either of these is happening you'll know that the ball is not going straight up. It should be halfway between you and the wall.

Now stand sideways to the wall and again toss the ball. Does it tend to lean towards the wall or away from it? Once again your ball is drifting. It is not being pushed straight up as it should be. Practice this exercise whenever you can until you develop the proper toss. It will help you gain confidence on the court.

Incorporate into this exercise your natural service stance and place your racquet on the ground, at a spot just off your right shoulder and 15 inches in front of your left foot. Make your toss. If it consistently reaches the proper height and lands on the strings, you are doing well.

The proper height for the toss cannot be overemphasized. It is so crucial to a good service. If the toss is too low, you will be shortchanged on the power that a fully extended swing can provide. You also will be minimizing the angle that the ball needs to be able to clear the net and still drop into the service court.

If the toss is too high, the service rhythm must, of necessity, be disrupted. This is sometimes referred to as putting a hitch in the swing—because you have to wait for the ball to descend. It becomes much more difficult to bring the racquet's sweet spot into contact with the ball when it is descending rapidly rather than "hanging" in the air.

Of course, strong wind can play havoc with a high toss, throwing the entire serve out of whack.

I would make it a practice to work on the toss as part of the overall service motion. After reading and absorbing the chapter on the swing mechanics, you can add the following method for synchronizing the action. You don't need a ball or a racquet. Just think it out. Move slowly at first. The entire motion will become rhythmical as the pieces fall into place.

Without a ball or racquet extend your left arm as if you were pushing the ball upwards. Simultaneously, start your "rocking" motion or weight shift and go into the backswing. Now imagine giving the ball one final push with your fingers. Then, pow. Follow through.

Varying the Toss

Depending on the type of serve you are using, you will have to vary slightly the position of the toss, just as you have to alter the grip a bit. Once you have absorbed the techniques and concepts of all the service motions, you should practice with the most effective toss for each.

The Toss for the Other Serves

For the American twist serve, the ball should be thrown, almost directly overhead and just slightly in front of you. This will enable you to put a heavy topspin on the ball, the primary characteristic of the twist.

In the flat serve, the toss should be approximately 18 inches in front of you. It should be in line with your right eye rather than your right shoulder. This position change is dictated by the fact that you are not swinging the racquet to your right around the ball but hitting through it.

When the grip is changed even slightly from the Eastern towards the Continental, the ball tends to move to the left. To compensate for this, you toss the ball to the right, aim right and press in the same direction a bit. These are intricacies with which you will eventually come to terms after you've mastered the timing behind the toss.

I have emphasized practice techniques for the toss because it is probably the last thing one truly learns. Frankly, some players never are able to master it. It is a somewhat unnatural motion. Holding a ball on the tips of your fingers and pushing it

(1) The toss is too far from my body. It would land a yard or more to my front and I would end up chasing the ball. This is a bad toss. Balance and proper weight shift are lost. I would no longer be in control of my service motion. On the other hand, if my toss was slightly behind me, I would end up hitting the ball with just my arm, and my shoulders and body would be unable to lean and turn into the ball.

(2) The toss is too low. I would not get the advantage of full extension of the racquet. My arm would be cramped and I would lose the angle down into the service court so necessary for a good serve.

(3) A perfect toss. It is the right height, I'd be able to extend upward and outward to the ball and hit through it without stretching or cramping my arm.

upwards in a straight line to an exact spot without fail time after time is a challenge, to say the least. Practicing it is also rather dull. It's much more fun to get out and play a few sets.

But the toss is a vital part of the game and your fun will be enhanced and more victories gained if you have confidence in it.

At a Volvo International Tournament at Bretton Woods, one morning, prior to a match, I saw Jeff Boroviak all alone on the court. With racquet in hand and a ball he stood at the baseline for approximately 25 minutes doing nothing but tossing the ball up and looking at it, letting it bounce and then tossing it up again. Never hitting the ball, simply trying to get the feel of exactly where his toss was in relation to his body. Admittedly this must have been very boring, but Jeff did very well in that tournament. Practice will help to make for perfection.

In learning to vary the direction and speed of your serve, it is helpful if you don't have to move the position of your toss too much. Just as the grip on your racquet can telegraph your strategy, so can the toss. Try to prevent your opponent from "reading" your tactics.

Many players will signal a wide serve to the forehand side, for example, by tossing the ball further to the right than usual. Signalling in this way can nullify part of the edge such a serve can give you. You can be sure that a good competitor will be able to analyze it. Bear in mind that you may be giving your target area away if you move the toss around too much.

6

The Swing—

and Serve
Strategy

6

The Swing— and Serve Strategy

Of course the final component in the service motion is the swing which brings the racquet into contact with the ball and completes the serve. This must be coordinated with the toss which we discussed in the previous chapter.

The three basic serves, as previously indicated, are the flat serve, the slice or spin serve and the American twist serve.

I strongly advocate the slice or spin serve for all players who have progressed past the novice category. I do not mean, however, that you should depend on this to the exclusion of the others.

Let us first discuss the slice serve since it is the one I do recommend for players who have mastered other points of the game. I also recommend an economical backswing be applied with this serve. Do not try a big, sweeping backswing, that can only hamper your timing. In a long match it can also tire you.

The Locomotive Motion

From the ready position the simplest and best way to serve is to pull your racquet straight back and then up and around your head for the backswing rather than dropping the racquet head down into the usual pendulum type swing.

I call this a locomotive motion because it resembles the movement of the piston drives of the old-time locomotives. Dropping the racquet head to your ankles in the pendulum motion tends to loosen the swing too much. As I have said I like the tightness of a good serve.

My feeling is that the motions Roy Emerson goes through— three loops, dropping the racquet then pulling it back, wastes much energy. I can't deny that Emerson has certainly been one of the outstanding players of our times but as I've pointed out, don't try to emulate the top pros. What works for them will not necessarily work for you. So remember that the backswing is to put your racquet into the prime position. It is not a build up of power and you will not be significantly increasing the strength of your serve by taking a larger backswing. The strength of your serve will come from the "snap-the-whip" motion and your follow-through.

On the backswing, what you are basically doing is bringing the racquet back past your head with the racquet face properly slanted, your elbow bent slightly and your wrist firm.

As you start your backswing, your left hand will remain next to the throat of the racquet for just a second whereupon

76

This is the reason I call my method of pulling the racquet back at the start of the service movements the locomotive motion. It resembles the piston drive motion of a steam locomotive, few of which are seen today. Pulling the racquet back in a pendulum-like motion is not wrong. A majority of players, including some of the greatest, use it. It is just that I believe the locomotive action conserves energy. In a long match this extra energy may be the deciding factor.

that hand, holding the ball, will drop slightly to help pick up momentum. At this point you should be starting to arch the racquet up towards your shoulder. As your right arm rises with the racquet, your left hand with the ball should also.

As you pull the racquet back, with its head slanted up, your right arm should be back around and over your shoulder. It should be a fluid movement climaxed when you have reached the slot at the top. The motion resembles that of a person about to scratch an itch with his right hand on his right shoulder blade.

If you'd like to see whether or not you are doing the scratch-the-back position correctly, try doing it as you look at yourself in a full-length mirror.

When your arm concludes the locomotive movement in the backswing and starts to pull the racquet over your shoulder, you begin to turn your shoulder. At this point your entire upper torso becomes involved in the swing. Your shoulders should turn from a position parallel to the net to one almost completely perpendicular by the time your racquet reaches the "backscratching" position.

Your right shoulder should now be several inches lower than your left. There are two reasons for this: 1) Your left arm is tossing the ball and at this moment should be reaching full extension. 2) Intentionally dropping your right shoulder enhances the coil of your upper body. This together with the cocking of the elbow, wrist and the bending forward of your legs provides for optimum spring into the ball.

Make sure you have the deep bending action for your legs. It is a natural response to the coiling of the rest of your torso, even though your knees are flexed at the onset of the service motion. At the top of the backswing your legs have reached maximum thrust potential.

The Prime Position

When we discuss the "prime position" we refer to that position you are in when preparation is completed and you are ready to make contact with the ball. As you move your right arm up on the way to the prime position, your body weight should be shifting back to your right foot.

As your right arm reaches its zenith and is about to drop into a cocked position, your left arm should be fully extended and the ball released. It is at this point that your body weight will begin its shift to your lead foot. As the ball rises to its zenith your right arm, with ever increasing speed, drops into the cocked or prime position. It is stationary for a fraction of a second and then explodes out towards the ball.

When you have completed the backswing you will be in the coil or prime position. Your elbow and wrist will be cocked, your back arched, your knees flexed forward and your weight is being transferred to your lead foot.

In the prime position.

79

Forming A "W"

The motion and coordination of your two arms into the backswing is often referred to as forming a "W" from the center of the letter since this is the path traced during the first part of the swing. Synchronizing the motions of both arms is not easy and requires a good deal of practice. Even the slightest miscue in timing will result in either (a) waiting for the toss to come down, thus putting a hitch in your serve or (b) not having time to get the racquet into the cocked position and rushing the serve.

Practice Without A Ball

Practice the locomotive swing pulling the racquet straight back, then up and around your head. At first practice it without the ball. Get the feeling, the rhythm of the swing, as you pull your racquet back and over your shoulder. Feel the flow of your arms from the center of the "W" at the ready position down very slightly through the two curves of the "W." Once you have this perfected, combine it with the toss. At this point don't worry about following through. Just practice the backswing with the toss, practice forming that "W" with both arms.

Now review all the movements in the backswing. Break them down and make a checklist. Write them out.

Your wrist must be kept firm throughout the backswing. It is only as the racquet is being dropped into the backscratching slot that the position of your wrist will change. As your elbow cocks down into the prime position so will your wrist, allowing for maximum snap.

Many people believe that the wrist should not be rigid through the windup. They reason that since the wrist should be loose when you're swinging at the ball it might as well be loose during the backswing. I don't go along with this. Too many players who loosen their entire swing tend to lose control. Keep your wrist firm during the backswing so that the rest of the swing will have a certain tightness. Most players will have better control of their entire serve if they limit the flexibility of their wrist to the point at which they are actually swinging the ball, just before impact.

When you initiate your swing and reach the full extension of your arm and the racquet makes contact with the tossed ball, your body will be fully extended upwards.

This action is like an explosion with a snap-the-whip effect where one action triggers another as all components come together in a smooth, rhythmical series of movements.

The Follow-Through

We now come to an important action of the serve which, surprisingly, seems to throw many players who have advanced beyond the beginning stage. That is the follow-through. Follow-through is very important, and once the player realizes how natural it is, the problems created by not following through are corrected. A good follow-through is often the crucial element in a good service.

Let me tell you what I feel is the best way to describe the action on a good follow-through. Once you have made contact with the ball be sure to throw the racquet face as far out as possible. Don't worry about pulling the racquet down over the ball. This will happen automatically when you can no longer throw the racquet out any farther. The limit of your arm stretch will pull the racquet down into a natural follow-through. Too many players, once they've made contact with the ball, feel that they must *pull* the racquet down if they are to put the ball into the service court. Not at all. It is an automatic motion once your arm is out as far as it can go. The only direction it can then take is down.

There are some pitfalls, however, to watch for on the follow-through. Many players, once they've made contact with the ball and after snapping their wrists, will halt the progress of the racquet in midswing while it's straight in front of them. What happens then is: (1) The loss of a good deal of power. (2) Expending extra energy in the course of stopping the racquet. One reason this is done by some is the player thinks he can control the ball better, that he can guide it better. This is also not so. After you practice your follow-through you'll find that following through all the way really gives you greater control. Otherwise you will end up with a patty-cake serve. An important point to remember about the follow-through—make sure that your racquet flows past the left side of your left leg, not your right. If your follow-through takes the racquet past your right leg, you are probably not turning your shoulders properly.

Another major point to watch is that crucial wrist snap. Many players who should know better will keep their wrists completely locked throughout the follow-through. You should snap your wrist for several reasons: (1) It can add a good deal more power. (2) It is the motion that puts the greatest part of the spin on your serve. It contributes to the topspin and the side spin.

The Explosive Serve

When the ball is tossed, your weight is transferred to your forward leg, your torso including your shoulders will be returning to a position parallel to the net, your elbow will be snapping up and out. Then comes the whip of the wrist, all culminating in an explosive serve. The ball should be hit at the top of the toss with your racquet fully extended.

It's hard to pinpoint the exact moment when each movement starts as all parts of your body are moving very fast. As noted previously think of it as a snap-the-whip effect. The first movement of one action immediately triggers the start of another—body weight shift to torso to shoulders to elbow to wrist. Each is an entity in itself yet inseparable from the whole. Because of the unity of this exploding motion I believe the best way to learn it is to imagine yourself as a baseball pitcher throwing your racquet up and out towards your opponent rather than a ball.

Where to Strike the Ball

To find the spot on the ball that you should strike, think of it as the face of a clock. As you swing through with your angled racquet face, try to make contact at about two o'clock and then brush slightly around it as you hit through. This puts that slight cradling effect into action. It puts the spin on the ball.

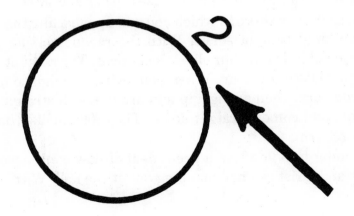

Practice your serve by performing the motions without a ball. Don't release the racquet, of course, but swing it fast enough so that you hear a whoosh of air through the strings. Once you can do this satisfactorily, combine it with the toss, hitting the racquet through the ball. At this point don't worry about hitting it into the service court. Just get the feeling of the motion. I can't stress the importance of this enough.

A Common Fault

One common fault that some tennis players, especially women players, have is that they don't allow the chain reaction to happen. There is no snap-the-whip effect. These players stand with their shoulders and torsos parallel to the net. They end up muscling the ball by using just their arms to hit it. Realizing that this doesn't produce much power, they throw their butts out towards the back fence as they hit the ball. They do not use their shoulders and torsos to turn into the shot. This also results in not using their body weight.

If you find you are doing this, practice throwing the ball in a pitcher's motion, without a racquet, making sure that your shoulders and torso are turning sideways and you are using that motion to start your elbow going through and your wrist snapping through. If you find you can't throw the ball properly you won't be able to serve it because the motions are the same.

Another poor serve in which you end up muscling the ball is the windmill type of serve. With the racquet in the prime position behind you, your elbow is not bent. The racquet sticks straight out to the rear. When you swing through to hit the ball your arm then swings up and around, still straight, hits through and comes straight down. The effect is like that of a windmill arm.

In doing this you lose a great deal of power because your elbow and wrist are not snapping out at the ball. Without the wrist snap you cannot put a spin on your serve. Not that you won't be able to put this type of serve where you want it to go. There are many strange variations to the serve but few produce winning games.

One player I knew would toss the ball in back of his head at about eye level and starting with his arm at his side would hit the ball. He looked like a chicken flapping its wings. Yet the serve went in. But he had no chance of maximizing his percentage of in shots. To maximize your chances of putting a serve in, you should hit the ball at the top of the toss with your racquet fully extended. At this point the angle into the service court is at its greatest, and by snapping your wrist you'll put spin on the ball. The more spin you have the more control you have, the greater the spin the quicker the ball will drop into the court.

If you are starting to learn the basic mechanics of the swing, practice by holding the racquet at the throat instead of at the handle. With a slightly lowered toss practice the service motion from the prime position. Get used to the feeling of making solid contact with the ball. Don't worry about how far it goes. Also get used to the feeling of the cradling motion. Think about what you are trying to accomplish with the slice. Choking up this far on the racquet will definitely help you gain control of the entire service motion. As you feel more confident, slowly move your hand down the racquet and continue practicing until you are all the way down the handle to your normal grip.

Some Additional Pitfalls

There are a few additional pitfalls you may encounter in mastering the swing. Watching some weekend tennis players I noticed that they often failed to open the face of the racquet as they dropped it into position. To prevent this from happening, make sure when your racquet is in the scratched-back position that the lead edge, the one not touching your back, is pointed somewhat out towards your right side. This will hold the racquet face in a slightly open position.

When you are practicing it is a good idea, every so often, to pose for a moment at the conclusion of your stroke. Observe where your right foot has landed. It should have moved directly forward towards the net exactly following the direction of the serve. There is an inclination on the part of some players to move their foot towards the right. This can throw you off balance and makes it difficult to catch up with a return to your left.

Placing the Ball

Where should you place the ball on your service? The most important goal in any serve whether to the deuce court or the ad court and no matter what the playing surface, is to put the serve deep in the service box, within a foot or two of the service line. It's not the speed of your serve that will hurt your opponent, it's the depth. Try not to have a shallow landing in the service court.

A lot also depends on the strengths and weaknesses of your opponent. Most beginning and intermediate players have a weaker backhand than forehand. You should then serve towards the backhand. If, by chance, your opponent has a stronger backhand then by all means serve to his forehand.

Most players serving into the deuce court will usually serve towards the backhand. This prevents the receiver having a good angle for his return. Therefore try to hit towards your opponent's backhand, keeping the angles for his return to a minimum. Most likely he will try to return the ball down the line towards your left side or straight down the middle. He'll have a problem going crosscourt to your forehand with his backhand. (See diagrams).

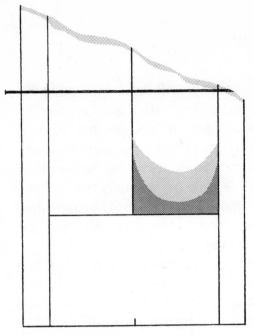

☐ *Less desirable area.*

■ *Optimum area to serve into.*

Areas to which to serve. The least desirable area in which to place the ball is the white area since the receiver will have better angles to hit back. See legend under diagram for better areas.

Another very effective tactic, one I use more often than any other, is to try to serve straight into my opponent's body. This tactic was used by both Arthur Ashe and Manuel Orantes to beat Jimmy Connors in 1975. They played the ball into his body where his angles of return were minimized. It's very difficult to make a good return if you have to move out of the way of the ball by backing away and are not able to step into it.

So, serving into the receiver's body, like serving towards his backhand, minimizes the angles he has to make his return. Basically he must hit down the center of the court.

Serving to Your Opponent's Forehand

This situation changes when you serve to his forehand, especially if you serve wide to his forehand. This serve opens up the receiver's crosscourt return possibilities increasing his angle for the crosscourt dramatically. With a good crosscourt return he can now pull *you* outside the doubles line of your court on the right side, which puts you at a distinct disadvantage. Unless he has a weak forehand, serve to the forehand only for a change of pace. Serve wide occasionally just to keep him honest. If he notes that you always serve to his backhand he will probably start to cheat over to that side. At this point you will want to go to his forehand.

The exception to a wide service to the forehand occurs if you are playing on a very fast surface. On these surfaces the ball tends to stay low, and to skip when it hits the ground. Your opponent will now have to hit up taking away most of his crosscourt advantage.

Serving to the Ad Court

In serving to the ad court, your strategy should change a bit. Again, depending on your opponent's weakness you will want to serve into his backhand which means serving towards the singles sideline of the service court.

The reverse now applies regarding his angles of return compared with the forehand court. Even though you will be serving into your opponent's backhand his angles on this side are improved. Even so, if the backhand is your opponent's weakness you will still want to serve to it even if the angles have increased slightly in his favor.

Here, too, serving directly towards his body is a good idea. Once again his angles will be very small for making a good return. That which held true for the deuce side holds true for the advantage court in serving into his body.

I do not recommend serving often down the line to the ad receiver's forehand. Even though his angles for return are not good, you are still probably serving to his strength. Again, serve to his forehand only for a change of pace to keep him honest, and from cheating too much to his backhand side. Occasionally serve down the center line to the ad player's forehand, if he's a receiver who likes to run around his backhand. Many players will do this, especially on a second serve, hoping to get in a strong offensive forehand shot and take the advantage away from you. If this happens don't hesitate to serve down the center even on a second serve. While he is running towards the doubles alley to use his forehand, your center serve will be far from him. You may even have an ace from what is a relatively weak serve.

Always do everything you can to get your first serve in. Don't give your opponent the edge we all feel when a player has missed his first and we expect the weaker second serve. Keep up the pressure. Your goal should be to get in at least eight out of ten first serves.

When you have to resort to a second serve remember to add a bit more spin. Forget the disadvantage in that it will be softer than your first serve. If the ball lands deep it doesn't matter. One advantage of the added spin is that you have a better chance to clear the net. The rules for placing the second serve are basically the same as for the first. Aim the ball at your opponent's weakness, probably his backhand.

The Flat Serve

I'd like to explain why the flat serve is so difficult to consistently get in the service box. With the flat serve you have no side or topspin on the ball. You do have a slight amount of under spin. Under spin tends to make the ball rise, just as the opposite occurs with topspin. When you hit a flat serve, your percentage of getting it in is therefore lessened considerably. With a flat serve the ball is actually rising. It has to clear the net and still come down into the service court. You see how precise you have to be.

There is very little margin for error with this serve, and for that reason I don't recommend using it often. You may have seen Roscoe Tanner using the flat serve. He's very good at it, but some days he may not get more than 50% of his first serves in because he is having an off day. To get a flat serve in consistently you must have a good day. Your timing has to be perfect. That is why I recommend the spin serve. Your margin for error is that much greater. Another reason the flat serve is not as effective as a spin serve is that most players receiving have more difficulty with a serve that is spinning away from them or spinning into them than with a serve that is coming straight at them or one that doesn't change direction.

Just as the spin service has been likened to a baseball pitcher's curve ball that drops, the flat serve can be compared with the straight overhand knuckleball, one of the hardest pitches to control.

The basic preparatory motions are the same for the flat serve as for the spin—the backswing, the scratch-the-back position, the coiling of the body, the cocking of the elbow and wrist. The difference is mainly in the actual position of the racquet at impact and the toss of the ball, which is more towards the center of the axis of your body.

At the top of the swing, you should be leaning directly towards the net. It is mandatory that you reach your fullest extension in the flat serve.

There will be relatively little spin resulting as you uncoil and uncock your elbow and wrist to meet the ball squarely. These must uncock just before you hit with the momentum carrying your right arm down and across your body. The follow-through resembles that of the spin serve.

You must have complete control of the racquet to pull this off, and the odds are against the average player using this type of service successfully on a regular basis. There is far more control with the spin serve.

There are, however, some very specific uses for the flat serve, even if it is only to eliminate a readable pattern from your service game.

The beginner will automatically try to pour it on with the flat serve, because it gives him a larger portion of the racquet face to deal with. He believes that even if he hits poorly, he will still be able to get the ball in, which is not so. He also no longer has to worry about compensating for the angle of the racquet face.

It is proportionately easier for taller players to use the flat serve. Their height allows them an advantage as to angle of service trajectory. They will not direct as many balls into the net as the player of average height.

The American Twist Serve

In serving the American twist follow the same directions for the spin or flat serve to put your racquet into the prime position. Use the locomotive action, pulling your racquet back, around and over your shouder.

At this point the American twist differs from the other two serves. In putting your racquet into the prime position you must arch your back severely. It is only by doing this that you will be able to put the necessary topspin on the ball which is the trademark of the American twist serve. If you don't arch your back you'll only put on a side spin.

With the ball almost directly overhead, your swing will come up and around towards your right rather than out towards the net as in the other two serves. With the racquet face almost completely open you will be making contact with the ball just about in the center, and then will be brushing the strings lightly up, over, and around the ball. You will be using a severe cradling motion. Although you will be swinging quite hard you cannot afford to hit the ball too squarely. If you do it will zip off the racquet before you have time to cradle it to put on the necessary topspin characteristic of the American twist serve.

You can hear the difference between an American twist serve, flat serve and even the spin serve. There should be much more of a brushing sound with the American twist. It is a quieter serve than the other two. There won't be the hard ping sound of the ball on the racquet. Once you have thrown the racquet out, around and over the ball, going towards the right all the while, you follow-through just as with the other two types of serves. Your racquet comes around and, as with the others, should end up going past your right leg. At this point your back has started to straighten and you can now get into your ready position or come to net behind the serve if you so desire.

When mastered, this serve results in a ball which should clear the net by a good margin thus assuring you of a high percentage of serves put in. It will also, when it hops, take an abrupt jump up and towards the left. This high hop will throw many of your opponents off their return of serve, especially if the ball goes into their backhand. These advantages, however, are counterbalanced by the fact that most players have a great deal of trouble mastering the American twist. It is difficult to do, given the necessity of arching the back. Then, when you arch your back, you give it away. The difference in toss also telegraphs to your opponent what is coming.

The Arm Motion

The motion of your arm in the American twist differs from the flat and spin serves. You do not come forward like a baseball pitcher. Rather you are throwing the racquet almost straight out to your right while your body is leaning into the net only slightly, unlike the spin and flat serves. It is not natural for these two parts of your body to move in different directions. The amount of pressure brought to bear on your arm is incredible and a goodly number of players have been sent to the sidelines with a prescribed layoff from extensive use of this shot.

I believe in the conservation of energy, and that is why I am not a great supporter of the American twist serve. Most "good" amateurs do not have the physical attributes necessary to execute this service. I also do not think it is worth the backbreaking (literally) effort which is needed to learn how to control it.

The American twist service is probably one of the major sources of tennis elbow, not to mention strained backs. Since most players cannot properly arch their backs in the required manner they attempt to muscle the ball with their arms and hands.

The toss for this serve can be either directly overhead or somewhat towards your left shoulder blade. With that great arch in your back, your racquet is dropped farther down than on any other type of service.

Many fine players who desire to have a service with topspin adjust differently. Some players will change their grip to a backhand and hold the racquet perpendicular to their arm position. They toss the ball a bit forward of their heads, then have the right edge of the racquet face leading through the shot as it moves straight up and over the ball before snapping through.

When you have progressed to the point where you are able to control the spin serve and are able to occasionally surprise your opponent with a flat service and augment your repertoire with a delivery that carries a bit of topspin, you have all the attributes necessary to move out of the intermediate class.

One Stroke at a Time

I should caution you not to move too fast. It pays to "walk before you run." Work on one stroke at a time. Gain confidence in it before moving onto the next. Take pains in increasing your command of various strokes and situations. You'll find it will increase your confidence in your ability to put over that winning serve.

You should stick with the spin serve no matter what playing surface you're on. On slow clay courts the chances of getting an ace are relatively small anyway so just make sure you get your first serve in and get it in deep. The controlled slice serve is best for this. Don't try to fight the playing surface.

When you are on clay don't try to hit the ball harder because the court is slower. Instead take advantage of the surface. Go for good positioning. Force your opponent into the least opportunity for making his best shot and try to obtain the weakest possible return.

Don't expect to win the point on your serve. Just set yourself up for the next shot. This is *so* important. Getting your first serve in on clay is even more important than on a faster surface. There's no sense in missing your first serve in an attempt to ace your opponent.

On a faster surface such as grass or hardcourt you may, on occasion, want to go to a flat serve. But again, just occasionally, for a change of pace.

Once you have conquered the problems that go with learning the spin serve and are able to put it where you'd like eight out of ten times, you should be pleased. You might then want

Too many players only practice their serve into the deuce court. Do practice from both sides. The angle that you will be serving into differs from the deuce to the ad court. Remember the height of the net varies depending on the side into which you are serving. There are many variables so practice your serve from both sides. Remember the name of the game is consistency and playing the percentages. Get your spin slice serve in deep and you'll take the advantage away from your opponent.

to move on to some variations on this same theme. Try putting even more slice on the ball by tossing it a bit farther out to the right and several inches more in front of you. Cut the ball and watch it fly out to your left. This serve provides a very good change of pace. Use it once in a while to pull your opponent out of court. This serve can open up his backhand side for you.

Correcting Errors

Perhaps you now find that you are hitting the ball into the net more than you feel proper. Raise your sights then and change your target area. Aim deeper into the service court.

If, however, most of your serves are going too deep, the way to correct this is by pushing your toss out a little bit further perhaps by only two or three inches. This should be enough to pull your serve down into the service court. Experiment, move your toss around. Discover the best place for your toss. You do have a general guide as to how far out it should be tossed but find out exactly where it should be for you. The results should guide you. But remember, don't try to put the ball into the service box by pulling down on the racquet before it has reached its full extension.

On the pages that follow you'll find detailed photographs of the movements in the three basic serves.

The Three Basic Serves

Spin Serve —
Front View

(1) The ball is held lightly between the thumb and first two fingers. My knees are slightly flexed and the racquet is starting to be drawn straight back. My head does not drop down at all. My weight at this moment is mostly on my rear foot; my left arm holding the ball is starting to dip prior to being raised. (2) The racquet is being drawn around and behind my head. My shoulders have turned and are almost perpendicular to the net. (3) The racquet is at the top of the back position. ready to drop into the prime position. The ball has been released. My knees remain flexed and my weight has started to shift to my front foot. At this moment my weight is evenly distributed. (4) The racquet is almost completely in the prime position. My shoulders have started to turn. My weight is almost completely on my front foot. Elbow and wrist are in the cocked position ready to snap through. On the toss the ball is slightly off my right shoulder. (5) The racquet has attained the prime position. It has completely dropped into position with wrist and elbow cocked. My shoulders are starting to turn back into the ball. (6) The racquet is not visible on the left side of the photo. Compare this with (5) in the flat serve illustrations. I will be cutting around the ball more than on the flat serve. (See next page.)

1

4

2

3

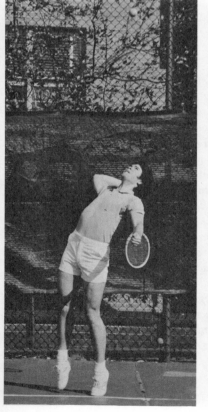

5

6

7

8   **9**   **10**

(8) My elbow is almost completely extended. My wrist is just starting to snap through. (9) You can see that my wrist has changed its position dramatically from the previous photo. In (8) notice that as the racquet is about to meet the ball it is not completely open. It is at an angle of about 45 degrees. Also, in this photo notice the full extension of every part of my body. (9) The ball has left the racquet which now appears completely open as it starts to pull towards the left. This is the cradling motion mentioned in the text. My eyes remain on the ball at all times. (11) My right foot is starting to cross over the line past my left foot as I begin to move into the court and up to the net. In (11) through (15) notice the change in wrist position as it completes its snapping through motion. This is a very important part of the serve as it gives the greatest spin to the ball. In (12) through (15) notice the way the racquet curves around the right side of my body. This differs from the flat serve where the racquet comes down directly in front of my body almost following the line of my right leg. The spin serve curves, like an arc. (15) Notice the way the racquet has come across my body and is trailing along my left side, ending its movement. Also notice how the lead edge of the racquet is now the racquet's bottom edge. It is part of the cradling motion and necessary to put spin on the ball. My weight has now completely shifted into the court onto the right foot.

100

11

12

13

14

15

Spin Serve — Side View

1

2

(2) The ball is held lightly between the thumb and first two fingers. My knees are slightly flexed and the racquet is starting to be drawn straight back. My head does not drop. My weight is primarily on my rear foot; my left hand holding the ball is starting to dip prior to being raised. (3) The racquet is being drawn behind my head. My shoulders have turned and are now almost perpendicular to the net. (4) The racquet is at the top of the back position, ready to drop into the prime position. The ball has been released. My knees remain flexed and my weight has started to shift to my front foot. At this moment my weight is evenly distributed. (5) The racquet is almost in the prime position. My shoulders have started to turn. My weight is now almost completely on my front foot. Elbow and wrist are in the cocked position ready to snap through.

(Turn page)

3

4

5

6   7   8

(5-6) In the spin serve the ball should be approximately 14 to 16 inches in front of you. (5-8) Note the way my body leans forward with my weight completely on my front foot. (6) I am now in the prime position with elbow and wrist cocked, ready to hit the ball. (7) Just before contact my body is at its fullest extension. Note that you can see through the racquet which means that it is quite closed and little of the racquet face directed towards the ball. I should be putting a lot of spin on the ball. (8) The ball is leaving my racquet and I am starting the cradling motion. (10) See how far out I reach as I hit forward through the ball.

9

10

In these photos Deborah Stier demonstrates the technique of the spin serve.

(1) Deborah is in the starting position, her feet properly set, her weight mainly on her back foot. (2) She takes the racquet back although she drops the racquet face as many players do. This is not wrong—it is another way of serving. Her weight has shifted slightly and is evenly distributed between both feet. The ball is being raised and the racquet is moving into the prime position. (3) The ball has been released and the racquet is almost in full prime position. Deborah is ready to start coming through. Her weight at this point is now almost completely on her front foot, her back is arched and she is ready to lean into the ball. (4) Deborah's body is leaning into the court just before making contact with the ball. Her wrist and elbow have snapped through and her right foot is starting to come forward, passing her left foot, as she gets ready to move towards the net. Notice her full extension as she makes contact with the ball.

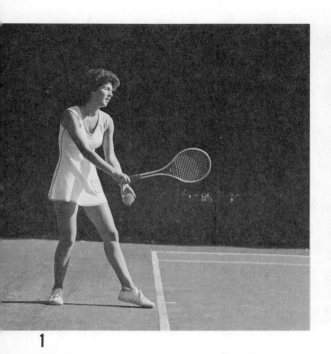

1

2

3

4

1

2

3

5

6

7

4

(1) Deborah in the ready position to start her serve. Her weight is primarily on her back foot. (2-3) She swings the racquet pendulum fashion before taking it back and over her head, and down behind her shoulder. She is also raising the ball for the toss. (4) The ball has left her hand and the racquet is coming up just before dropping into the prime position. Her weight is being shifted forward. (5-6-7) Deborah's racquet has reached the top of its swing and will drop into the full prime position. In (6) and (7) her hips and shoulders are perpendicular to the net. (8) The racquet has reached the full prime position and she has started the snapping through motion. Her body is leaning forward into the court. She is moving towards full extension and is a split second away from hitting the ball. Notice the cocked position of her elbow and wrist. Her hips and shoulders have started to come around to parallel the net.

8

9

10

11

(9) Just before making contact with the ball. Notice
that Deborah's eyes are on the ball the entire time.
Her right foot is moving forward, starting to pass
her left, so that she can move towards the net after
making contact. (10-11) The serving motion is completed and Deborah has stepped into the court.
Notice the way her racquet comes around the left
side of her body. She allows the motion of the
racquet to naturally spin out and does not try to
stop it.

Pancho Gonzales has just hit the ball. Notice the downward turn of his wrist as it completes its snap. Gonzales had what many people considered the finest serve in tennis. He always made full use of the extension of his body, hip and shoulder turn, along with elbow and wrist snap.

The Flat Serve

1

(1) The ball is held lightly between the thumb and first two fingers. My knees are slightly flexed and the racquet is starting to be drawn straight back. My head does not drop down. My weight is primarily on my rear foot; my left hand holding the ball is starting to dip prior to being raised. (2) The racquet is being drawn around and behind my head. My shoulders have turned and are now almost perpendicular to the net. (3) The racquet is ready to drop into the prime position. The ball has been released. My knees remain flexed and my weight has started to shift to my front foot. At this moment my weight is evenly distributed. (4) The racquet is almost in the prime position. My shoulders have started to turn. My weight is almost completely on my front foot. Elbow and wrist are in the cocked position ready to snap through. (5) The snapping through motion has begun. The racquet is moving towards the ball. Notice the way my elbow has started to uncock although my wrist is still cocked. My knees are unflexed and I'm on my toes trying to get a full extension up and at the ball. The racquet is visible on the left side of my body whereas in the previous photo it was visible on the right. This happens only with the flat serve because the racquet instead of curving around the ball must go straight at and through it. (6) My elbow is almost completely extended and my wrist has begun its snapping movement. My shoulders are now completely parallel to the net. Notice how my eyes are on the ball the entire time. (7) Just after contact. Both elbow and wrist are now completely uncocked. The racquet face is almost completely open. It is flat to the ball which will produce no spin. (See next page.)

5

112

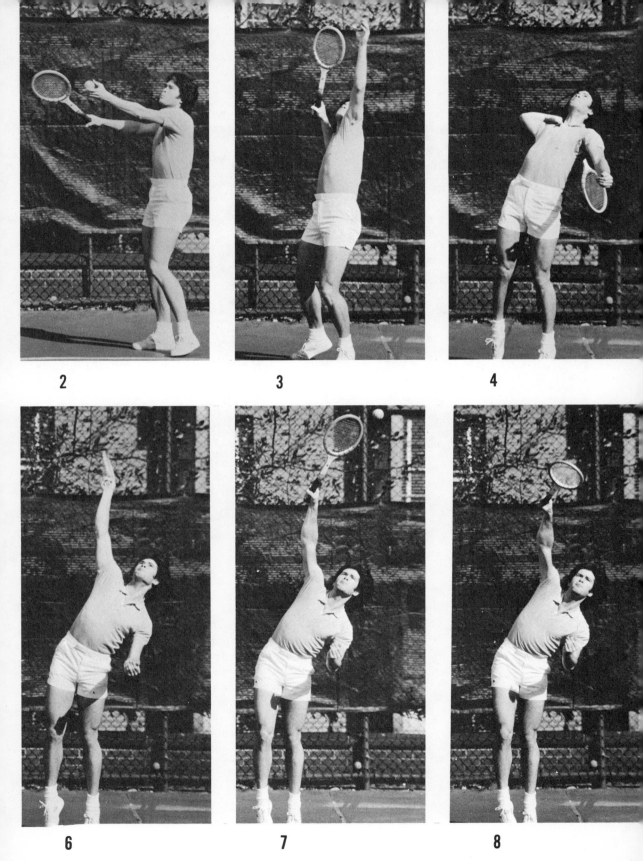

2   3   4

6   7   8

9

10

(9) *My right foot has started to cross over my left so that I can move towards the net. My wrist is continuing its snapping through motion and is now pointed downwards. (10) All the snapping motions have been completed and I am letting the racquet follow through with its natural momentum. Notice that in the last four pictures the racquet maintained a fairly straight line as it came over my shoulder around and through the ball. There was very little curving motion. This is necessary in hitting a flat serve. You must go straight through the ball.*

114

Margaret Court has made contact with the ball and both feet are off the ground. Her right foot is starting to pass her left so that she will be able to make her way towards the net. Notice the extension of her arm and racquet out and through the ball.

American Twist — Front View

1

2

In photos (1) through (4) the instructions are the same as for the Spin and flat serves. Note, however, that in (3) and (4) my back is starting to arch more than in the flat and spin serves. The ball is also not to the side of my right shoulder. It is farther to the left. As the racquet reaches the prime position (4) and starts to come through (5), it is visible on the right side of my body. This position is necessary in order to put the extreme top spin on the ball which is the mark of the American Twist. You have to cut around it. (See next pages.) In (5) through (7) note how my knees are never fully extended. In this serve they remain slightly flexed throughout the shot. Full extension is not a concern here since it would not permit the arching of the back. (5) Note the angle of the racquet as it starts to snap through.

3

4

5

(6) The racquet appears quite flat as it makes contact with the ball but it is actually brushing up over the ball. The lead edge of the racquet is pulled up and across the ball. Note also the position of the racquet after contact has been made. In the final three photos note the arc the racquet makes on an extreme circle to the left as the service motion is completed.

6

7

8

9

10

American Twist — Side View

1

2

(1) Note how my weight is on my front foot, the rear foot providing balance. Note also that the racquet never goes below my waist. It is pulled directly straight back. I always recommend starting the serve in this fashion rather than using the pendulum type swing since I feel it conserves energy. (2) My weight has shifted to my rear foot and in (3) and (4) it once again shifts to my front foot. This slight rocking motion is used by many experienced players. The other arm and body movements are similar to those in the spin and flat serves. Note that the ball is not tossed too far out in front.

(Turn page)

3

4

5

(6) and (7) My back is extremely arched and is leaning towards the left and the snapping through motion of wrist and elbow has started. (7) (8) and (9) Note the direction the racquet is taking as it moves towards the ball and following contact. It is not moving out through the ball as much as it is cutting up and rolling over and swinging out towards the right.

6

7

8

9

10

1

2

5

6

3

4

7

Here you see the similarity between the use of the racquet in serving, and throwing a baseball like a pitcher. Throwing a ball is good practice exercise to use when first learning to serve. (3) and (4) My weight shifts to my rear foot. (5) It shifts forward as my arm drops into the prime position. (6) Starting to throw out and through. Both elbow and wrist are cocked and ready to snap forward. My back is arched. Note the difference between (5) in which my shoulders and hips are perpendicular to the net, and (6) in which they parallel the net as I start to turn my body.

125

The ready position for the serve is similar to the ready position of a pitcher just before he winds up. Notice the similarity in foot positions.

Just as in the game of golf, in tennis you should meet the ball off your lead foot in front of you.

126

Hitting a tennis ball in the return of serve is similar to hitting a baseball. Both have a characteristic turning of the hips and shoulders. The racquet has been taken to about five o'clock for the forehand shot. My knees are flexed, head is low so that I am almost on an eye level with the ball. Both racquet and bat are comfortably close to my body for better control.

Billie Jean King has one of the best serves in tennis. You will be able to observe her technique and movements on the next three pages.

Photo on opposite page: She tosses the ball up, her racquet is ready to drop into the prime position and her weight is leaning towards her front foot. She is ready to start the snapping motion.

On the next page: Her racquet has swung through the ball. Her eyes are still on the contact point and her right foot has come through and is into the court, enabling her to make her way to the net without wasting time. Her wrist is still being snapped.

Last photo: The racquet is perpendicular to the ground and Billie Jean's wrist has completed its full snap. Notice how far she leans towards the net.

7
Return of Serve

Something that has always surprised me in reading most tennis instruction books is the lack of information on return of serve. I imagine that most writers, and also instructors, lump the return in with their teaching of the groundstrokes.

Anyone who has played a reasonable amount of tennis will quickly realize that the return and the groundstroke require two distinct approaches. To my mind, the return of serve is the single most difficult shot in tennis. It is the exact opposite of the serve in that it is very often defensive in nature; it is the countering of what must be considered an offensive weapon —the serve.

There are exceptions, of course, to this view of the return as a defensive maneuver. To the world-class tennis player, the return is often seen as a chance to put the server in trouble.

Jimmy Connors is a perfect example of this. Connors' strong suit in my, and many other people's opinion, is his return of serve. With remarkable accuracy he hits it as hard or harder than the serve he is receiving. He intimidates his opponent rather than vice versa. By hitting hard, well-placed returns, Connors steals that supposedly innate advantage the server has. It is the server who freezes for that vital instant and hesitates at the moment of return. It is the server who is wary and tentative. It is the server who is lunging and stretching for his first volley or initial groundstroke.

The returner is confident, in control, and on the offensive. What Connors does is to get his opponent *thinking*, not in the positive sense, but in the nervous, doubting sense. Connors won't let his opponent simply react, won't allow him to play "unconscious," "out of his head," or "in the zone." Connors makes him consciously work to hold his serve.

If you can take the inherent "gimme" nature out of your opponent's service game, you will be making him work about twice as hard throughout the match. There will no longer be the pattern of easy game, hard game, easy game, hard game; every game will be a struggle. That added pressure will eventually crack most opponents. And the lever, the crowbar, with which to apply that added pressure is the return of serve. It is for that reason that Connors has been number one in the world. Now, admittedly, I have been talking about world-class play when I speak of Connors. But even the average player can learn to dramatically improve his or her return by changing the concept of what a return should be, where it should go, and how it should be hit.

I am assuming that you have a basic knowledge of the two groundstrokes, the forehand and backhand. Any return of serve, of course, will require the use of these.

Jimmy Connors' return of serve is his strong suit.

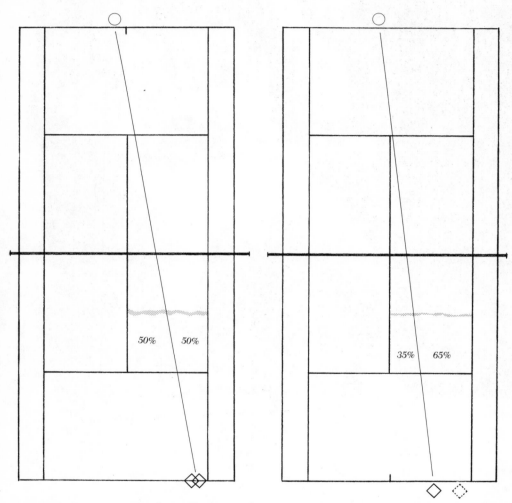

50%   50%

35%   65%

Position for receiver who will return in singles. Note that the returner has drawn an imaginary line from the server to himself and divided that part of the service box nearest to him approximately in half. (Double diamond is receiver.)

In this diagram the receiver has shifted his position to the left because the server, noting his opponent's weak backhand, has been consistently serving to that portion of the service box. The receiver has reduced the area for a successful serve to his backhand.

Where to Stand

The first point to consider in returning a serve is where to stand to give you an equal opportunity to make either a forehand or a backhand return.

There is a standard receiving position which most people use. It is just behind the baseline approximately 6 inches to the left of the singles sideline when you are receiving in the forehand court and 6 inches to the right of the other singles sideline when receiving in the backhand court. This leaves your opponent no real advantage in trying to serve to either your forehand or backhand since you are in a position to return either shot with equal facility.

For the most effective position, however, look at the spot on which your opponent is standing for his serve. Then position yourself so that if you were to draw an imaginary line from his position to your position it would bisect that portion of the service box closest to you. (See diagram.)

Adjusting Your Position

Under certain circumstances, however, you may want to adjust this position. If, as is true with many average tennis players, your forehand is considerably stronger or more consistent than your backhand, you may want to cheat a little bit in your positioning to draw the serve to your forehand.

For example, you're receiving in the forehand court and during the match your opponent has managed to get his serve into your backhand fairly often, causing problems for you in making your return. Shift your position one or two feet to the left. You have now considerably narrowed his angle towards your weak shot, the backhand, and "invited" him to challenge your confidence shot, the forehand. If he still attempts to get his serve into your backhand, let him. The reduced angle will significantly decrease his percentage of accuracy and the number of first serves he makes. You have forced him to alter a heretofore winning strategy and are making him work harder. You are making him think and hesitate, not letting him play to his own rhythm.

Against a Powerful Serve

There are other variations to this positional shift in different situations. Against a very powerful serve, try standing a foot or two behind the baseline. This will afford you further time to react and to 1) recognize where the ball is going, and 2) get your racquet back into position so that you can swing into the ball solidly with good balance. A rushed return in which your whole body is jerking upward in an attempt to pull the racquet around in time is generally disastrous. You need time to remain low and establish at least minimum racquet momentum for a firm, solid return.

Against a Weak Serve

Against a weak serve, a second serve, or a high bouncing (heavy topspin) serve, it might be wise to move a foot or two in front of the baseline. Against a weak serve, this will let you cut the ball off quicker, thereby rushing your opponent. It will also allow you to make contact with the ball at the top of its bounce rather than when it is dropping, thus maximizing your margin for error in putting the ball over the net. Lastly, those few feet closer to the net increase slightly the angle, and therefore the percentage, for a crosscourt return.

Not only do these three reasons for moving closer to the net hold true for the high bouncing serve but in addition you will want to cut off this type of serve before the bounce forces you to stretch. Stretching reduces the control that is present when the racquet is closer to your body.

The Grip on the Return

What is the best grip to use for your return? It varies and there are many theories. Top players the world over are divided on the subject.

Many players change their grip from forehand to backhand and vice versa in making their return. This practice is fine if your opponent's serve is relatively slow in pace and/or if you react remarkably fast. Many people I teach find this switching technique confusing and it is the cause of many a bad return. The reaction time to a reasonably well-paced serve is comparable to that for a volley. There are plenty of players who are easily capable of confidently executing solid and consistent groundstrokes, yet these same players when placed at the net to volley or behind the baseline to receive a serve act as though their racquet has turned from a wand to a club. They flail, jerk, and worst of all, panic.

Using One Grip

To help yourself overcome this fear of the return, you have to convince yourself that you are not being rushed, that you have the time to react positively. And indeed you do have the time. When you are learning to return the serve use one grip, the Continental. It will help support this feeling of added time. Just as most instructors will advise their students to volley with the Continental, I likewise recommend it for the return until you have become quite expert. Every tennis student has heard when learning the volley, "You won't have time to switch from one grip to another." I have found this holds true on the return as well.

Take a look at some of the similarities between the volley and the return of serve. On both, it is not always possible to get your feet into the proper position; very often you'll find your feet parallel or only slightly shifted (having not had the time to "step into the ball"). If this last is true, it is again true in both cases that you'll be making the return (or volley) with a redirection, a countering, of your opponent's power. Since you don't have the balance or body position to hit the ball back as hard or harder than it comes at you, you have to use your opponent's strength against himself. It's the same concept found in Judo, turn your enemy's aggression to your own advantage. To attempt to do more on the return is difficult, tiring, and unnecessary. Also, on both volley and return you will not be using a full swing but something more abbreviated, more a punch. So, use the Continental, until such time as you feel confident in changing grips. It will let you hit off both sides (backhand and forehand) without being concerned about the proper grip.

Changing Grips

When a player has passed through the intermediate stage and is better able to judge his opponent's service, he will be better prepared to shift his grip. If you have reached this stage, you can now think about grip changes.

A good deal of the way you grip your racquet also depends on the strengths and weaknesses of your opponent as well as your ability to combat his service. You most likely will not react the same way in the first set of a match as you will in the last, since other variables have been added—score, stamina, concentration.

If you find that your opponent is serving frequently to your forehand you might try adjusting your grip a bit towards the forehand (Eastern) grip. If the serve is coming to your backhand more frequently then you might shift it more to your backhand side.

When you are in position and awaiting the serve, your feet should be parallel to the baseline and about two feet apart for good balance. Try to keep on your toes. Don't stand there flat-footed. Many good players will shift their weight from foot to foot and finally bounce up onto their toes just as the ball is being served to insure that they will be alert and able to react quickly in any direction. If you are keeping your weight on your heels during this anticipatory period, then you cut down by a split second the amount of reaction time between serve and your return.

The Crouch

I'd like to say that not enough emphasis has been placed on the crouch while awaiting a serve. This is one time when a player has the luxury and the time to ready himself to such an extreme. The crouch enables the player to set up on the balls of his feet. Gird to spring laterally in either direction or move forward or back as the situation dictates.

The crouch also allows him to get a better bead on the ball, just as when a batter in baseball crouches at the plate his eyes are more on a plane with the pitched ball. It is particularly important with a curve ball, since it enables the player to calculate the speed and amount of spin being produced. This applies to tennis as well. The crouch also gives you a lower center of gravity which, in turn, gives you greater balance. The more balance and the better base you have, the better you will be able to return a fast ball than if you stand up straight.

Secrets of A Winning Serve and Return

Cradling Your Racquet

Cradling the throat of the racquet in your left hand can be significant in several ways. Most important is that in returning the serve, with the ball coming at you fairly rapidly, using your left hand to pull the racquet face back will be much faster than if you take it back with your right hand alone. Taking it back with your left hand enables you, by feeling the flat end of the throat, to make sure the hitting side of the face of the racquet is in the position you want it to be, perhaps just slightly open (facing slightly upward).

Using your left hand to draw the racquet back can also force you to turn your shoulders. This is especially important on return of serve where you may not have the time to turn your feet, and so the leverage achieved from the turned shoulders is very necessary.

Many times I've seen players who take their racquet back and once back the racquet face is completely closed when they don't want it to be. This occurs because when the racquet face is in back of their bodies they tend to lose any feeling for the position of the face. Your left hand placed on the throat can help keep the racquet face in the proper position. Use of your left hand in this way can also prevent you from taking the racquet back too far. It acts like a barrier preventing you from wrapping the racquet all the way around your back. Remember, on a return your swing is going to be shorter than on a normal groundstroke, and your left hand will help shorten your swing.

Racquet Level

In a similar vein, many players facing a hard serve, and taking their racquets back quickly, automatically bring it up too high. It may be a reflex action, but it happens. Although it

142

depends upon the type of return they want to make, they'll probably have to lower their racquet. This takes valuable time. In this, situation if you're trying to hit your return straight through with a little bit of underspin, bringing the racquet up high and having to drop it takes up valuable time. Use your left hand to help keep your racquet at hip level unless you plan to bring it higher. If so, use your left hand to do that. Your left hand acts like a starting gate when you cradle the racquet this way. When you're ready to swing through, pull the racquet out of your left hand like you'd pull a sword out of a sheath. If you do this you should have no problem completely controlling the racquet face. It will be in the same position as when you were cradling it. You'll be able to swing through with a great deal of confidence with the help of your left hand.

When the Server Is Rushing the Net

The receiver should not allow the server to rush the net and take control of the situation. The best way to combat this is with a swift, short chip shot.

This chip return is similar in form to the return you make when you move closer to the net against a weak serve. With it you'll be cutting down on your swing and attempting to just punch it back.

One of the highest percentage of effective returns is found when you can chip the ball over the center of the net which is approximately six inches lower than at the sides. You may well ask, "If I hit it down the center am I not hitting it right to my opponent?" Perhaps, but if your shot is low, at his feet, his angle of return is restricted. He does not have much court to work with.

If your return takes your opponent to the sides of the court, either forehand or backhand, he then has angles which tend to maximize his chance for a put-away shot if your return is net level or higher. Therefore it is highly desirable for your return to be a low shot which minimizes his angles. Hitting down the middle with a low shot is a very sensible return, and you'll have a high percentage potential of making a good return and putting your opponent in trouble.

The receiver must also punch the ball back as soon as possible, when it is close to its apex. The reasons for hitting the ball at this point is that once again the angle is improved and you will make your return before the server is able to get close to the net. The faster you can make your return the farther back he'll be and the more room you'll have for making a low return. If he's almost on top of the net by the time you make your return it's hard for you to do much with that shot. There is no time for a backswing on this shot, but if your timing is right you have a good chance to handcuff the server before he reaches the net.

As mentioned before, only the server is aware of the type of shot he is going to deliver. But the receiver also has a certain advantage. He can be sure that the serve will have to be placed within the very defined limits of the service box. There is plenty of time to get set, to stabilize the grip, put the racquet at the ready and be positioned in the most desirable stance . . . ready to move in either direction.

Concentration Required

The return of the service may be the stroke in tennis which requires the most concentration since the ball is coming from a completely different angle than most other groundstrokes and the spin also varies considerably. Although it is imperative for the receiver to always keep his eye on the ball, it is more urgent that on the return the receiver follow the sphere and actually view it making contact with the strings of his racquet. It has been suggested by some, and I don't think it a bad idea, that the receiver actually attempt to visualize a spot about the size of a pinhole in the exact center of the ball. This does one positive thing . . . it forces you to concentrate on the return, not the machinations of your opponent.

Don't be distracted and turn your eyes even for a split second. If your opponent is rushing the net, you will know it. You can then proceed to try to direct the ball past him on either side, hit a low sinking shot at his feet which he will have to volley up, or you might deftly lob over his head. If your opponent is not rushing the net, the best shot will most likely be deep and away from his strengths.

Make it easy on yourself. Be sure you've made contact with the ball before you start to run towards the net if that is your strategy. Your body should lean slightly towards the net and towards the ball so that your shoulders and torso once again are able to turn into the return of serve.

Playing in a championship tournament at Innsbruck one recent summer, I found many of the contestants did not come to net following their serve. Being European they played in the European fashion relying on a baseline game, and their opponents would stay back and rally with them.

My best strategy was to try to cut the ball off early on every second serve and even on some of the first serves and get up to the net. This put a lot of pressure on my opponents. They weren't used to seeing someone coming in. As a result, they made quite a few errors. If I had stayed back and rallied with them, these would not have happened. They were comfortable with their own kind of game, but not with a forcing game where one comes to the net. Remember, getting to the net puts a lot of pressure on your opponent. If his shots are not accurate you have a put-away shot.

The Second Serve

If the server faults on his first serve and is on his second, it is almost certain to have less speed than the first. Punch it quickly at the center of the net which is the lowest point.

Running Around a Serve

Since, as previously indicated, most players have a stronger forehand than backhand, it not only implies that we must practice our backhand with great dedication, but that we should use our forehand in a match and perhaps run around a serve as much as possible. Remember, however, if you are going to improve you must work on your backhand.

When you decide to run around a serve, to hit it with your forehand, it is better to do it in the deuce court, rather than the ad. If you run around the ball in the ad court you'll find yourself outside the doubles lane. Unless you hit a terrific shot that your opponent is unable to return or that really puts him in trouble, he will then have the entire court to hit back into. In the deuce court you will be running towards the center of the court and thus putting yourself in a better position.

Analyzing Your Opponent's Serve

If you are able to correctly predict the nature of your opponent's service, you will have more time to prepare for the return stroke, be able to set up better, follow through more effectively and control your stroke while hitting the target. A champion tennis player begins moving for the serve before it is over the net. His racquet will already have started moving back.

This advantage is gained by utilizing the percentages and the knowledge of your opponent's tendencies. If you are well disciplined and are truly able to concentrate on your game, you will know that given a certain score, knowing a definite

146

pattern that has evolved through the match, you should be able to come to a valid conclusion on the direction and type of serve that will be offered.

The more experienced player will weigh the intangibles such as fatigue in a hard, close match and the way his adversary reacts under pressure. This type of "reading" comes only through experience.

The intermediate player, however, can and should be able to anticipate by observing his opponent's habits throughout the course of the match. It is not that difficult to decipher and takes only a little study. For example—the server's position at the baseline, the height of his toss and position. Is it directly overhead, far to the right or somewhere between?

If the toss is overhead, you can assume an American twist service and know the spin on the ball will be heavy. If the ball is tossed well away from his body (to the right) it will almost definitely be a wide slice serve which will cut to the right. The closer to the body the toss, the flatter and harder the resulting service. From these few clues, you should be able to predetermine his method of attack.

Know Yourself

One good way to analyze your opponent's approach is to know yourself a bit better. If he is in the same playing bracket as you, he will most likely react the same way. Don't forget, as an intermediate player he does not have all the shots in the bag at his disposal. A good way to anticipate the kind of return on the second serve is through the process of elimination. Would your opponent, for example, try an American twist or difficult flat service after he has already had one fault? Not likely.

Most probably he will slow down, toss the ball out to the right and attempt to get a good slice service into the court, allowing for a pretty good margin for error.

This is no guessing game. It is putting to use your observations and conclusions as to your opponent's strengths and weaknesses, his dependence on a certain stroke in a crucial situation and his emotional and physical state. Then use them to your advantage.

The Strokes To Use

What kinds of strokes should you be taking in making your return? In a great number of cases, the speed at which the serve is coming at you will not permit you to take as full a stroke as you might with a regular groundstroke. If you have the time, fine. However, in most cases you probably won't be taking a full stroke. This is made up for by the fact that in returning a serve you will be using the speed put on the ball by the server. You do not need to provide that speed yourself.

If you are able to take a full groundstroke swing against your opponent's serve, by all means do so. That is, if you feel you have the time to do so. I place a good deal of emphasis in this chapter on what to do when the rate of speed of the serve is such that you cannot take a full stroke. If, however, you do have the time for a full stroke, the sections on the placement of your return and other aspects of the return are the important ones for you. It is also important to study the sections that deal with situations in which you do not have time to place your feet correctly and take a full swing. You will often be faced with these.

Another point in playing doubles is to try to keep your return strokes short, which is not too different from what you should be doing in the singles game. By keeping your strokes short you will not give away the direction of your shot as easily. It will keep your opponents' net man frozen in position for that fraction of a second which will be helpful in putting the ball by him.

148

Use An Imaginary Clock

The following should be somewhat of a guide for your return stroke. Imagine that you are standing on the face of a huge clock with twelve o'clock in front of you at the net and six o'clock behind you. When you make a return either from the forehand (deuce) or backhand (ad) side of the court your racquet should never go back farther than five o'clock. When the serve is coming into your backhand your racquet should not go any farther back than seven o'clock.

Depending upon the speed of the serve coming at you or the type of playing surface you may want to shorten these return strokes even more. You might, for example, take the racquet back to three o'clock or two o'clock when you're making a small punch return from the forehand. From the backhand you might be making it from nine o'clock or ten o'clock. These shorter strokes will be used against the faster serves when you don't have the time to take a greater swing. Bear in mind that the bigger the swing the less control you have of your return.

Take into account the surface you're playing on—grass, wood, a hard court or any of the mat surfaces—these are quite fast. You should then cut down considerably on your return stroke. Your return should be from perhaps four o'clock on the forehand and eight o'clock on the backhand. If you are playing on a slow court such as composition or clay, or some of the slow mat courts, take a slightly larger swing.

No Time to Shift Your Feet

In many instances, upon receiving a very hard serve, you will not have the time to shift your feet at all. In this case simply turn your shoulders. If you keep your shoulders parallel to the net your return will be made using just your arms. Few players are strong enough to make a good return with their arms alone. If you turn your shoulders back into the shot you will have twice as much power, twice as much solidity in your return.

Remember, also, to move your lead foot in if you have the time but it is not mandatory. It is, however, I repeat, mandatory to turn your shoulders, even if just slightly, so that your body can help your arm make the return.

Remember, too, that your wrist should be rigid. It does not break. Your elbow, however, will break slightly as you punch out through. Your arm should be close to your body and as you make contact with the ball it is pushing out, punching out through the ball.

Cut the Ball Off on a Diagonal

When a ball is coming to you, high on your backhand or forehand, it is important to try to cut it off on a diagonal in front of you at about ten o'clock on the backhand and two o'clock on the forehand. If you don't you'll meet the ball at your side. You will then use your wrist to bring the racquet around which will not produce a solid shot. Move over and up and cut these shots off. Taking them at the side of your body means that you'll get none of the leverage that you have when you shift your body into the ball. So try to take them in front of you.

Placing the Ball

Where should you try to put the ball on your return? There are a number of factors to be considered.

From the forehand (deuce) court, when the server stays back and is not coming to net, your return should try to clear the net by two to three feet. There is no percentage in trying a shot which just skims over the net. When your opponent is back don't try to get depth on your shot by hitting it back hard. Get depth by clearing the net by several feet. Wait until you get into the rally.

If your opponent is coming up to net you might have to make a better shot and just clear the net. When he stays back, however, you have plenty of room to work with. In this situation, there's no need to risk an error. Maximize your chances to give yourself the highest percentage and clear the net by several feet. Probably the best place to hit is right over the center of the net.

If you feel that you can do a bit more with the shot, go down the line. Here again you'll have a fairly large rectangular area in which to hit.

Hitting down this line should also put the shot into your opponent's backhand, which, in most cases, will be his weaker stroke.

If you're playing in the forehand court and your opponent is coming up to net, what do you do? This is the time to hit a topspin shot, if it is in your repertoire. It's a very good shot because it drops low quickly and will make your opponent volley up towards you. However, an underspin shot is just as viable. The easiest shot to hit is the one that goes down the center, right at the player.

At this point you must be aware of several things. If you decide to try to hit down his alley when he comes to net, you must remember that he has a very good angle with which to volley crosscourt and he will pull you out of court. (See diagram.) If you do decide to hit down his alley, remember to run quickly to the center of your court to be able to cover his crosscourt volley should he do so. Don't hit the ball and just sort of move back easily towards the center. Get back quickly.

If on the other hand you decide to hit crosscourt to his forehand volley, you have eliminated the extreme angle that he has on you. He should not be able to put this ball away on you very easily, because once again you have reduced his angles. (See diagram.)

Summing up, from the forehand court when the server is coming to net your two best possible returns are down the middle, low or crosscourt, low. You may want to adjust these returns depending on your opponent's forehand volley as compared with his backhand volley. If his backhand volley is not as good as his forehand volley you may want to hit in that direction even though you'll be leaving yourself more open.

Returning from the Ad Court

If you're returning from the ad court (the backhand court) and the server is staying back, the same rule applies as for the deuce court. Clear the net by several feet, hit deep and try to keep your opponent back. That reduces his advantage. Again your percentages are the greatest if you hit directly over the center of the net or slightly crosscourt to his backhand. If you hit down the line, it will most likely be to his forehand, presumably his stronger side.

If the server is coming up to net from the ad court your best shot again is low, down the middle over the lowest portion of the net and next best, slightly crosscourt to his backhand volley. This last leaves him no appreciable angle. No part of the court is especially open. However, returning crosscourt in this fashion, you also have less court to hit into. (See diagram.)

If you do hit down the line, of the three possible returns, this gives you the lowest percentage. If your opponent can return

(Continued on page 157.)

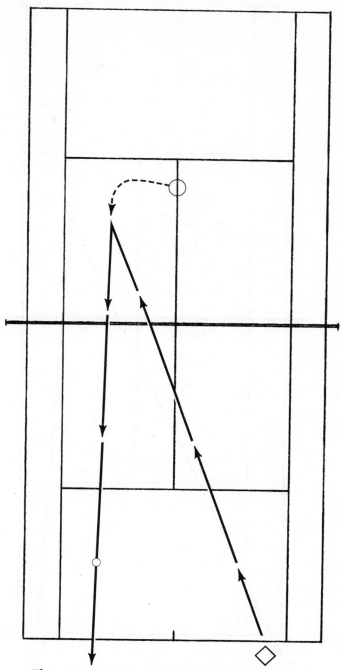

The crosscourt return when the server is coming up to net. Circle is server. In this situation the receiver has cut down the possible angles of his opponent's volley.

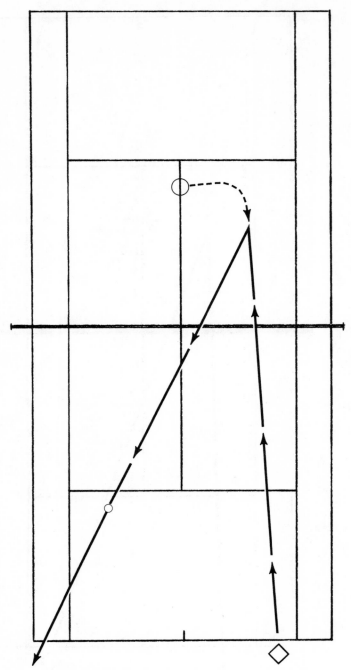

By returning down the line the receiver has en-
hanced the angles for the server to hit crosscourt
and pull his opponent out of court. Circle is server.

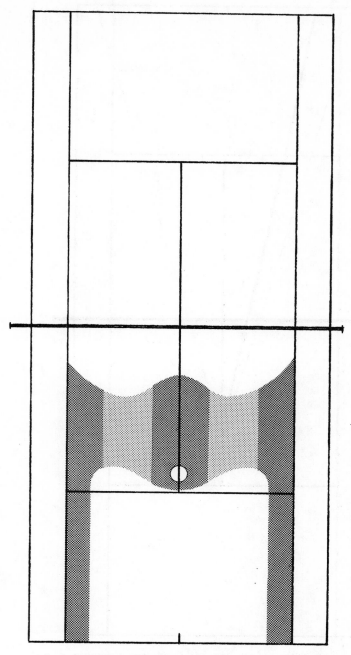

The best places to put a return. When the server is coming to net hit low at him or put in dark shaded areas which are optimum. If hit in light shaded area, ball must be low to be effective.

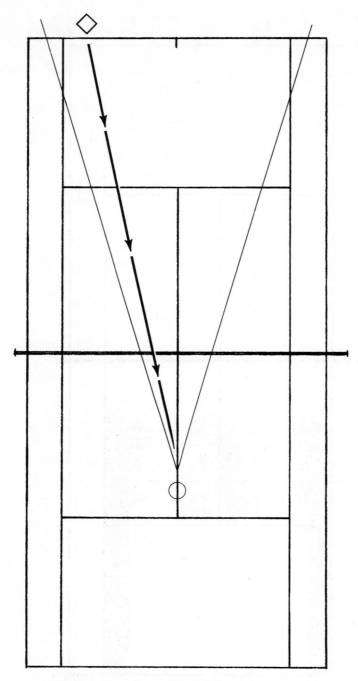

Return—hitting down the middle at server coming up to net. Black lines show angles server then has.

the ball with his forehand volley he'll have the entire right side of your court in which to place it. You may well be pulled way out of court, if, indeed, you get to the ball at all. If you do decide to hit down the line to his forehand volley with its greater return area for you, try to put the ball as far from him as you can. Otherwise you'll be quite vulnerable.

If the server is coming up to net at a very rapid pace from either the ad or deuce court, and you have been returning poorly, and perhaps your confidence is low, your best strategy may be a lob. It is the easiest to get back over the net. If you can direct it to your opponent's backhand side, he'll probably run around to try an overhead smash from his forehand which will be awkward for him.

Keep all of the above principles in mind and you'll find yourself having a greater percentage of successful and effective returns.

The photographs that follow illustrate the various kinds of shots you should be taking on the return of service.

Forehand Court —
Flat Forehand

1

2

This is the type of return with which I feel very comfortable. At the back of its swing the racquet is only at about five o'clock. In using a flat forehand return do not take the racquet too far back. Since you are hitting flat it means you are putting added speed on the ball and you do not need a big swing. Note my bent knees and the shoulder and hip turn. (3) through (7) The racquet face is flat as (Turn page) it makes contact and comes through with a very slight pulling motion upward so that I can give the ball a slight bit of lift over the net. (5) Note that I meet the ball in front of my body and I'm not taking it at my side. This is very important. Never let the ball pass on your side. In front you have a better view of the ball and its relation to the court. If you don't take it in front you will be pushing instead of hitting the ball. This return is effective on a ball that is a comfortable distance from you, neither too wide or too close.

3

4

5

6

7

8

Forehand Court — Topspin Forehand

1

4

(1) At its farthest point my racquet is pulled back to about six o'clock. My hips and shoulders have started to turn. (2) The racquet has started to come through and is at waist level. (2) and (3) The racquet face is flat and is meeting the ball solidly. In (4) through (6) my racquet has made contact and is coming over and pulling up. Note the racquet's arc throughout the entire serve. It eventually pulls up and over my head which imparts topspin on the ball. Also in the last photos you can see how my lead (left) foot is slightly to the front of my right foot. This gives that bit of balance needed to make the return, along with the turn of shoulder and hip. Most players feel more confident hitting a topspin shot with their forehand than they do with their backhand. The topspin forehand shot should be hit from a comfortable position or even when you are pulled quite wide. It is difficult to hit if the ball is too close to your body.

162

2

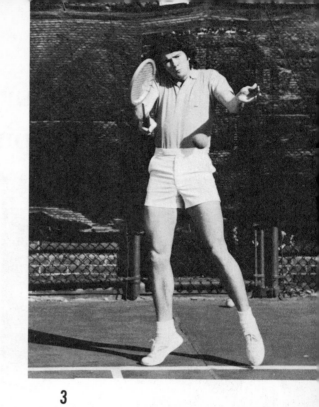

3

5

6

Forehand Court —
Underspin Forehand

1

2

3

4

(1) Note the way my shoulders start to turn. At this stage they are almost completely perpendicular to the net. This is one of the most important aspects of the return, turning your shoulders and also your hips a bit. The racquet is slightly over my head because I will be cutting down through the ball to impart underspin. (2) Ready to come through the ball. Notice how my racquet is not in back of my body but is at approximately a five-thirty position on an imaginary clock. I'm not taking an overly large swing. The ball is crowding me a bit so I push back onto my left foot. Yet I still keep my shoulders turned and my hips slightly turned also. (3) through (5) My shoulders and hips are turning back into the shot. The racquet is dropping a bit and its face is extremely open with a slight upward tilt. (4) Just before contact with the ball, note how every part of my body is very tight. Even though I look a little crowded I'm in complete control of all body movements. (5) The racquet head is below my waist as it moves in a cutting down motion. The downward arc with an open racquet face puts the underspin on this return. I did not have time to move very far. But because I moved backwards onto my left foot and turned my shoulders and hips I put a reasonable amount of strength into this return.

165

5

Forehand Court —
Topspin Backhand

(1) My left hand is on the racquet, preventing me from taking it back too far. It is at approximately six o'clock. My right foot is slightly in front of my left. This gives that minimum amount of balance necessary on the return. Also note the extreme turn of shoulders and hips. (2) (3) and (4) The racquet face is flat and open to the ball as I make contact. The racquet is pulling up through the ball. This imparts topspin. All during this motion my wrist is kept firm. I put topspin on by keeping the racquet flat and pulling up, rather than trying to flick over it with my wrist. This increases control of the shot and cuts down on errors. My knees are slightly flexed as I make contact. In the last photo as I raise my racquet I raise up. This helps put a little topspin on the shot. For this type of return you cannot be stretched out too far towards the ball nor should the ball be too close to you. You must be in a comfortable position to hit this shot with any degree of accuracy and in order to get it in.

3

166

4   1

5   2

Backhand Court — Topspin Forehand

1

This is the type of shot many players will run around to hit. On a ball coming towards your body you must move your feet and put your left foot in front. (3) My racquet is back to almost seven o'clock. In this way I am trying to make a very offensive shot. (4) The racquet is down, almost to knee level, which means that I will put a good deal of topspin on the shot. (Turn page.)

2

3

4

5

(6) As I make contact the racquet face is flat. My racquet is not too far forward. If it were more in front I would be hitting straight down the line. Here I am trying to return slightly crosscourt. (7) and (8) Following contact I pull the racquet up and over my shoulders.

6

7

8

Rod Laver is using the American twist

Backhand Court — Underspin Forehand

(3) (4) and (5) Note how the ball slides off the racquet with the underspin. Also note how I hold my arm back. In a doubles' return this is even more vital because you must slide the ball crosscourt to avoid the net man. This return crosscourt is one of the few times that you meet the ball at your side or even further back. It is impossible to slide this underspin forehand crosscourt if you meet it in front. (4) through (6) Note the slight downward motion of the racquet as I impart underspin to the ball. In the final picture the bottom edge of the racquet is leading through the stroke. This graphically illustrates the open face position of the racquet with a slightly upward tilt. This very versatile return can be used on a ball that is a comfortable distance from you, one that is pressing in towards your body, and even on a ball that is at a fair distance.

1

2

3

4

5

6

7

Backhand Court —
Underspin Backhand

1

2

The most common backhand return of serve in the game of tennis. (2) The racquet is back at about seven o'clock. It is approximately at eye level. The racquet face is slightly open until contact with the ball whereupon it is opened up to give maximum area for hitting. I still get the underspin because I am pulling down. Hip and shoulder turn throughout. (See next page.)

3

4

5

6

(6) I take the ball about 6 inches in front of me. This is absolutely necessary to make the backhand underspin return. You must pull around the ball and keep it in front of you. My elbow has remained slightly bent throughout to help control the racquet. With a fully extended arm you would tend to lose control. So, when possible, on underspin shots, keep your arm fairly close to your body. Don't throw the racquet way out. This return can be made with any type of serve.

7

8

8
Doubles

Playing with a partner is a whole new ball game, if only for the fact that you must take into account the assets and liabilities of a person other than yourself.

Although the rudiments, the stroke techniques and mechanics remain the same, the mental approach in doubles differs drastically from that in a singles match.

One basic decision to make when you begin playing doubles involves judgment—the selection of a partner. In choosing a doubles partner, try to pick someone who will complement your own game. If you are not a big hitter but fairly steady, then you should look for a partner who is more of a power player. That is—someone who can make put-away shots, who can end a point, whereas you'll be the one who is setting him up.

One reason my father was very successful with two different partners, Gardnar Mulloy and Tony Trabert (they were ranked #1 in the U.S., respectively, 7 years and 1 year), was his consistency. With good placement he was able to set points up for his stronger partner.

If, however, you're a strong player who can dominate the game, the best partner for you is one who is very steady and can get every ball back.

The same situation applies to women's doubles. Find someone who complements your game, one who can do the things that you can't.

There must also be a healthy relationship between the partners, one born of mutual respect. I have seen far too many partners haggling after losing a match, attempting to pass the buck and placing the blame on the other guy. This is not the way to go.

After choosing a partner, you must decide which of you is going to play the deuce court and which the ad court. The stronger player, the power player, should play in the ad court. This is to put his strength, most likely his forehand, in the center of the court. When he is at net his forehand is towards the center and he will be able to cut off the balls he poaches with his forehand. If your partner is left-handed, don't automatically cede him the ad side, as most people unthinkingly do. Remember that a leftie playing the ad side when at net will have his backhand exposed on shots down the center of the court. As a team, you will not have a forehand covering the center of the court, where most shots will go. Therefore, experiment to discover your capabilities in such a rightie-leftie marriage. Does the combination of his volleying and returning combined with yours provide a better balance from the ad or deuce court? Try both and weigh the results.

Doubles Setup

The usual doubles setup is to have to two playing partners in a diagonal formation in which the non-serving partner is at the net on the opposite side facing the receiver. There is another formation used, the Australian or Aussie. In this setup, the net man lines up on the same side of the court as the server like a "I" formation in football. Here, after the serving partner has struck the ball, he runs diagonally crosscourt to the net to cover that area. He must cover what would have been his net man's area in the traditional positions.

If your opponent is returning your serves crosscourt with great precision and power, both with his forehand and his backhand, this Aussie formation may be an excellent strategy, if you find you're not able to handle these returns. By lining up in this Aussie formation, your net man is now in his direct crosscourt path.

If your opponent now hits crosscourt he'll be hitting the balls directly to your net man who is in a better position to put them away.

What you are doing now is forcing your opponent to hit down the line. The chances are that his down-the-line shot may not be as good as his crosscourt shot since he most likely has not practiced the line shot as often.

Also, in this fashion, you may be breaking up his rhythm and throwing him off mentally. If he is not able to do what he usually does, you may have taken the edge away from his game by forcing him to do something he really prefers not to.

In the Aussie formation the net man should be approximately one to three yards back from the net (depending on your ability to cover your half of the court) and approximately one to three yards to the side of the center service line.

If the receiver tries to hit crosscourt with the net man in this position he'll have very little room to hit into. Try it. Line up in this formation and see how little room there is (a small triangle) into which your opponent can try to hit. Almost every other spot can be covered by sticking your racquet out. If he can hit into this small area where the net is highest and the area smallest, let him do it.

It is mandatory in doubles that you and your partner take the net. At the net you have many different angles and directions in which to hit the ball. Unlike singles where one can be bypassed when at the net, in doubles, with only nine feet added to the width of the court by the doubles alleys, two players at the net should be able to cover the entire area.

Therefore, it is highly desirable, perhaps imperative, to get up to the net as quickly as possible, thereby forcing your opponents into the backcourt. With all the angles to work you should be able to force your opponent into making errors.

Serving in Doubles

While it is very important to get that first serve in the box in a singles game, it is even more vital in doubles. You will want to join your partner at the net as quickly as possible. It doesn't matter how fast your serve is. As a matter of fact the faster your serve only means your opponent will receive the ball sooner and may well be able to return it before you have an opportunity of moving to the net. The slower you serve the more time you will have to get to the net. So, it is very important to get that first serve in. Spinning one wide off the court on the right side in doubles is also not as effective as it is in singles play. Doing so gives your opponent a better angle for a deep return.

Remember, in doubles you will not be serving from a point next to the center mark as you would in singles play. You may well be in a position five to seven feet to the right of the center line when you're serving to the deuce court and the same distance to the left of the center line when you're serving to the ad court. This enables you to cover your half of the court more effectively since you have the added area of the doubles alleys.

Don't concern yourself about the other half of the court. This is your partner's responsibility. What must concern you is being able to get to the ball if your opponent makes a wide return into your doubles alley. If you're standing too close to the center mark it's going to be difficult to get that shot. If you do get it yours will be a weak defensive shot. Therefore, stand farther over and cut off the angle of return which the doubles alleys give your opponent.

This, of course, does make it a little more difficult to spin a serve into your opponent's backhand in the deuce court. If you can, try to spin it into his backhand, but keep in mind that the most vital thing is to get it in.

There are times when you might find it necessary to stand closer to the center line. That is when an opponent is killing you with very hard crosscourt returns. It will enable you in this case to open up your opponent's backhand side in the service court giving you more room to hit into. And despite the disadvantage of being this close to the center mark, you do have the advantage of hitting to his weaker side, making for a weaker, and easier to recover, return.

Serving to the Deuce Court

In serving to the forehand (deuce) court in doubles, the most effective serve is one that spins the slice to the opposing player's backhand. Another effective serve is one that spins the ball directly towards his body. Either of these shots gives that player very little opportunity to angle his return. His most effective return will be one that is crosscourt. If the ball is going directly towards his body or to his backhand the opportunity to angle the ball in the crosscourt return is minimized.

If you hit the ball to your opponent's forehand, he has an extreme angle to work with.

If you decide to serve wide to your opponent's forehand in the deuce court, let your partner know that you'll be doing it since when your opponent is pulled out of court, one of his best shots will be to hit down your partner's alley. The further out he is the more the alley opens up for him. Make sure your partner knows so that he can cover his alley more intently.

Serving to the Ad Court

In serving to the ad court in doubles, if your opponent has a weaker backhand than forehand, the best serve is the slice serve in towards his backhand. Although this opens up the crosscourt backhand angle for him, just as in singles, it is likely he will not be able to utilize it. Here again, serving into his body is an effective shot. It too cuts down on any angle he has for making good returns.

Although you'd normally want to avoid his forehand when serving into the ad court, this shot is worthwhile not only for a change of pace, but for more frequent use. Once again when you serve down the middle of the court he has little angle to work with, none going towards the net man and he can't return it crosscourt to you very well. He probably will have to hit right back at you or down the middle, and you should easily be able to cover these areas.

In serving to the ad court you have a better choice of the kind of serve to use. You might utilize the American twist occasionally. If you find that your opponent has trouble handling it, use it a bit more often than just for a change of pace.

I don't recommend using the flat serve. It is not worth the risk of missing that first serve. If you put it in, the ball will reach your opponent quickly and his return will often be upon you while you're still behind the service line.

Returning the Serve

There is a great deal of difference between returning a serve in doubles and that in singles play. In singles you have a lot more room to work with in the court. Your opponent might not be coming to net. That takes a lot of pressure off you as a receiver. But in doubles there's always going to be a man up at net when you're receiving, making it necessary for you to make a decent return. If you pop a shot up or sail it lightly over the net, there's a good chance that the net man is going to poach and put the shot away. You don't have the luxury of clearing the net by several feet or the choice of which side of the court to return into. You have to return it on an angle, away from the net man. This necessarily limits you.

In the Deuce Court

If you are the receiver in the deuce court and the serve comes into your backhand, the best play to make as the server comes to net is to hit it directly back at him or off towards his doubles' alley. In other words, towards his forehand.

If you can, try to make the ball dip down over the net so that he has to volley up. This gives you a slight advantage. If you can make this type of return, you can come in behind and try a volley off his rising shot (or give your partner an excellent opportunity to poach). Do this only if you're confident that you've made a good low return and can get up to net fast enough to cut off his return.

The best return off a backhand in the deuce court is to hit it back low at the feet of the server who is coming to net, which means having the ball bounce somewhere in front of the service line. Chances are you'll be making this type of return with a certain amount of underspin for control.

If the serve comes into your forehand, whether wide or not, the shot to play is crosscourt, trying to put the ball at your opponent's feet. Possibly use a bit of topspin. The topspin will drag the ball down even quicker. It's a tough ball to handle for a player trying to make a volley. It has the added advantage of going in with a little more speed.

If you cannot put topspin on the ball, you might use the chip type of return, the underspin, which you've been making on the backhand side, using it with the forehand return, keeping it low.

In the Ad Court

If you are the receiver in the ad court, try to keep it away from the net man by returning it crosscourt. Another return to make from either side is to hit directly at the server rushing the net. Hit it with a bit of pace again, trying to keep it fairly low, but remember the harder you hit it the less the ball will dip down. Many players find this harder type of return difficult to handle but one of its disadvantages is that the ball, because it doesn't dip down, leaves your opponent better angled for his volley. Perhaps the added speed of the return will throw him off.

Alternate Your Returns

It is a good idea to alternate these returns and prevent your opponent from gauging your game and knowing the type of return you will hit in each situation. Occasionally hit one with a bit of speed, but remember this means he will have better angles with which to make his volley.

On a high return, if your opponent has the opportunity he'll hit his first volley straight at your net man. Having the ball dip low over the net helps prevent that and forces him to go crosscourt to you. You don't want to have your net man killed by a bad return off your racquet. However, if your opponent serves and charges into the net as fast as he can, before you've even made your return, it is very difficult to dip a ball down over the net. The best way to play him is to lob. A lob is a very good shot off a return of serve and not too difficult to control. If you are playing someone who serves and zooms in, hit a lob that lands as near the baseline as possible. The chances are that his momentum will carry him right past the ball, forcing his partner to cover for him. If he does get to it he probably will not be on balance to make a very good overhead shot. If he is smart he will slow down and adapt his game to yours—which is what you want.

Defense Against Poaching

Suppose you're playing against a team whose net man is constantly poaching? One of the best defenses or offenses against a team like this is the lob. Lob over the net man's head off either forehand or backhand. A high defensive lob, no real pace, placed over his head to land as close to the baseline as possible.

If you do this with any consistency it should force the net man to back up one, two, or three feet. Backing up takes away

187

part of his angle for cutting off your returns. He will no longer be as effective at poaching because he must now be concerned with playing his partner's balls. In both cases, if your lob lands anywhere near the baseline you should be able to come in behind it and take the net, which after all is the name of the doubles game.

However, don't only think of the lob as a defensive weapon. The lob is a very good offensive weapon if used correctly. If you are up against a team, one or both of whose members lean over the net to make their volleys, throw up those lobs and take the net away from them. Another way of keeping the net man honest is to occasionally hit down his alley, just hitting the ball through nice and easy. Make your opponents realize that you're not always going to return crosscourt, that they'd better be aware of the fact that you are able to hit down the alley. This should freeze that net man in his spot for a bit. It should cause him to think a bit longer, to wait and see where your return is going. If you can freeze him for that extra second, you will take a good deal of advantage away from a poaching net man.

The lob can also come in handy when you are not returning very well. If you don't feel confident about your return of serve, or if the server has a very hard serve, or an effective American twist that you are having trouble handling, use the lob. It doesn't take as much accuracy to hit a decent lob. You're pushing it into the air to get it deep. It doesn't require the precision that a normal crosscourt low return takes. Keep yourself in the point. Remember, in doubles making that return is essential. Kick it in if you have to. Once the ball is over the net you will have shifted the pressure from yourself to your opponents. They must do something with it.

Another return when receiving in the ad court is made by

running around your backhand and hitting with the forehand, if it is the stronger stroke. To do this effectively, analyze the serving habits of your opponent. Where does he usually land his second serve? If he tries to get it to your backhand almost every time, it's not too risky to run around it and take it on your forehand, hitting back crosscourt.

This is not so easy to do on the first serve since your opponent will be more confident and will mix his serves. He may also hit harder into your backhand, giving you no time to run around it. So this is more a tactic to use on a second serve. It is not so effective from the deuce court because in running towards the center of the court you open up your entire right side. If your opponent makes a decent volley, you may be in trouble. Don't give him this large angle. Running around a serve in the advantage court doesn't give him a large angle.

It is great if you have a net man who can intimidate the opposition. If the net man is within reach of a shot he should take it, because his return to your opponents will be so much faster than yours from somewhere around the service line. He can cut it off with a better angle. This forces your opponents and puts them on the defensive. If your partner is moving around at the net with the other side very aware of his presence they will be forcing their returns, cutting them that much closer to the net. This is hard on their confidence, on their mental preparation. If you don't know what the net man is going to do, you tend to be tense. Instead of relaxing and making your usual returns, you press more.

Remember, in doubles, the most important step is to get the first serve in, to allow your partner at the net the chance of making a put-away poach. If you can consistently get your first serve in, preferably deep, it'll give your net man confidence and put more pressure on your opponent to make a good return. If your opponent relaxes because he's facing a second serve, his confidence will go up and he'll make a better return. So keep the pressure on. Get your first serve in. Also make sure that you come up to net behind your serve. Don't stay back. Take the offensive, get to the net which is the winning position in doubles.

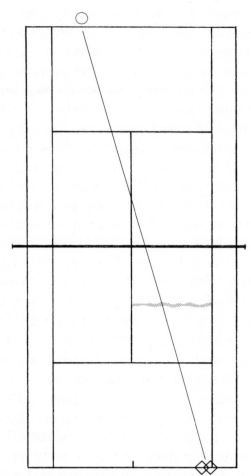

Position for return in doubles. Circle is server. Note that imaginary line divides near half of service box is divided in half again, lengthwise.

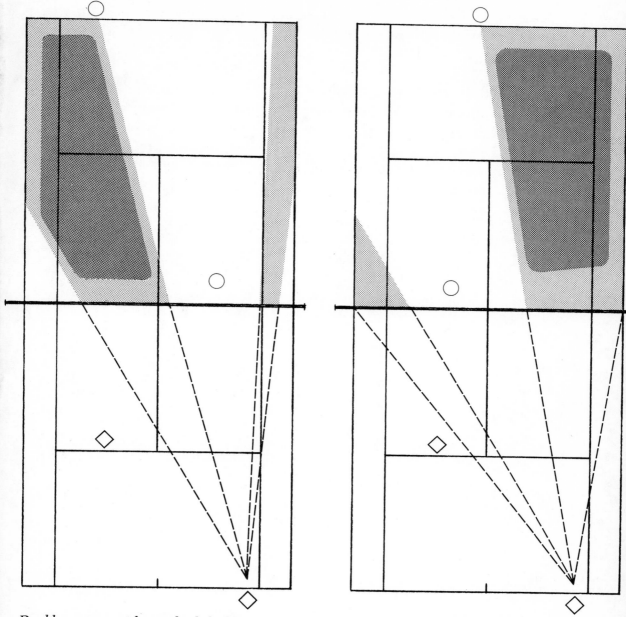

Doubles return with standard doubles forma-tion. Circle is server. Dark shaded section is op-timum area in which to return. Section in light shaded area, while desirable, has lowest percent-age of getting in.

Doubles return with Aussie formation. Dark shaded section is optimum area. Light shaded area, while desirable, does not give a high per-centage.